BEHIND THE WIRE

Behind the Wire: From Manila to Japan: A WWII Prisoner's Memoir

Copyright © 2025 by Richard G Lowe

Behind the Wire

RICHARD LOWE

CONTENTS

See books by Richard Lowe at
https://masterofworlds.com

Get free publishing insights and industry updates at
https://thewritingking.substack.com

For ghostwriting and book coaching services see
https://thewritingking.com

| 1 |

Authors Note

This memoir, "Behind the Wire," is the true story of Frank Hoeffer II, meticulously crafted from his personal journal, which he completed after the war, and a handful of informal interviews with his family. None of the names have been changed.

Frank's years as a prisoner of war were brutal. His words carry the anger he earned in captivity. That hatred toward his Japanese captors appears in these pages without adjustment. It is part of the historical record of what he endured, and it belongs here.

Content Warning and Disclaimer

This memoir contains graphic depictions of wartime violence, torture, starvation, disease, and death. The experiences described include systematic brutality and extreme physical and psychological trauma. Reader discretion is advised.

This memoir is based on conversations between the author and his grandfather, supplemented by his grandfather's original written account. While every effort has been made to ensure historical accuracy, some dialogue has been reconstructed from memory and some events have been dramatized for narrative purposes. The experiences depicted reflect one individual's memories of wartime trauma and should be understood within that context.

| **2** |

Prologue: Christmas Kitchen

The drive from Lake Arrowhead to Escondido was five hours of pure hell. My parents were arguing in the front seat about everything and nothing: money, directions, whose fault it was we were running late. My sister and I were trapped in the back, watching Southern California's incomplete freeway system crawl past while listening to another round of greatest hits on the car radio. Who spent too much, who didn't call ahead, who forgot to bring the right gift for whom.

Grandmother was waiting in the driveway before we'd even shut off the engine. She started complaining while our car doors were still opening. The suitcase was too heavy, we were later than expected, why didn't we leave earlier like she'd told us to? Her smile appeared instantly when she noticed someone might be watching from a neighboring house, then vanished the moment she turned back to us.

I fled immediately to the TV room, sinking into the big easy chair surrounded by her obsessions. UFO magazines scattered across every surface, Erik von Däniken's books about ancient astronauts stacked in towers, Buddha statues competing for space with alien conspiracy theories.

I'd read those von Däniken books cover to cover, all of them, several times over during previous visits. *Chariots of the Gods, Gods from Outer Space,* mysteries of vanished civilizations and ancient technology. I was seventeen, bored out of my mind, and desperate to disappear into theories about anything other than my family.

Christmas morning arrived quietly. Everyone sleeping off Christmas Eve tensions, the house finally still except for sounds coming from the kitchen. I needed to escape from that chair full of ridiculousness about visitors from outer space, from the atmosphere that had followed us across three counties. The kitchen offered refuge. No magazines about flying saucers, no family arguments, just the steady rhythm of someone working.

I found my grandfather already deep into Christmas dinner preparation. Standing straight as an arrow while dicing onions for stuffing. Every movement precise, practiced. Knives sharp, cutting board clean, and his ingredients arranged with military efficiency. He had the timing calculated to feed fifteen people without a single dish going cold, the kind of logistical planning that looked effortless but revealed decades of experience feeding hungry men under pressure.

The kitchen smelled like sage and butter, onions sweating in cast iron. Steam rose from pots on every burner. He moved between stove and counter without wasted motion, checking seasoning with a wooden spoon, adjusting heat with quick twists of his wrist.

My parents had mentioned he could be moody, made an irritating noise with his teeth, and kept to himself mostly. But watching him work, I saw something different. This man took feeding people seriously. He couldn't stand the thought of someone leaving his table hungry. The care was there in every careful measurement, every tested seasoning, buried under years of gruffness and distance.

Every few minutes, that sharp intake of air through his teeth. The sound that drove everyone crazy but seemed necessary for his concentration. His Navy posture never left him, even while stirring gravy or checking the oven. This was his domain, the one place where whatever had made him difficult transformed into something useful, something generous.

After the morning feast was finished and the dishes cleared, the family scattered to digest and complain about other things. We moved to the living room. The afternoon light slanted through windows, dust motes drifting in the warm air. He settled into his comfortable easy chair, worn brown leather that molded to his frame. I took one of those metal folding chairs they kept stacked in the hall closet, the kind with vinyl padding that stuck to your legs. The physical discomfort seemed appropriate somehow. I was the outsider here, the one asking for something.

"You want to know about the war?" he said, glancing at me while making that familiar sucking sound through his teeth. "It didn't start with Pearl Harbor for me."

What followed would take years of for me to fully understand. The stories came in pieces, fragments, sometimes prompted by a question, sometimes emerging from long silences. He'd pause mid-sentence to make that noise with his teeth, straighten his already perfect posture, then continue with some details about Shanghai or Manila or places I'd never heard of.

It would take several conversations for me to understand why he cooked with such fierce intensity, why he always made too much food, why he watched everyone's plate to make sure they ate enough. The abundance of every meal was his quiet rebellion against memories he'd carried for forty years without talking about them.

This man who couldn't let anyone leave his table hungry had once been starved nearly to death for three years and four months.

The conversations happened just in time. Years later, Alzheimer's would steal both the stories and the man who could tell them, but for those few Christmas visits when I was a teenager, his mind was still sharp enough to trust me with everything that had shaped him. While other family members complained about his moods and avoided his presence, I sat on that uncomfortable folding chair and learned what it meant to survive hell and emerge still willing to feed anyone who walked through your door.

These were the stories no one else had asked for. This was the inheritance no one else had wanted.

This was how I learned that feeding people isn't just kindness...sometimes it's the only way left to fight a war that never really ended.

| 3 |

Shanghai Nights

I was nineteen. Barely. Still carrying farm weight, broad but soft. They loaded me on a transport and shoved me across the Pacific. That tub stank day and night...diesel fumes, piss that never washed out, vomit rubbed straight into the deckboards. The whole hull lurched hard enough that plates rattled, teeth knocked together in our heads. My stomach never left my throat. Hell, I thought it might set up camp there.

The bunks were stacked three high, air close and sour. Hammocks rocked with every wave until they tangled like nets. Men coughed, groaned, whispered home names into the steam. The ship felt alive, bolts groaning, steel ribs grinding against the ocean's push. Every second smelled of rust, fuel, and men packed too tight.

Shanghai hit...hit like a swinging beam. Coal smoke, thick...thicker than soup, thick enough it clung behind your teeth. River water bubbling with garbage, sewage cutting sour through it. Spices, sweat, death all mingling. Rickshaws darting, vendors yelling prices, half a dozen tongues snapped sharp against each other. Japanese soldiers stood stiff at their posts, bayonets gleaming like polished glass, eyes pinned unblinking into streets that wouldn't rest.

And there she was. *USS Oahu.* White paint, striped awnings stretched taut, low in the river...looked more ferryboat than warship. But her flag cracked overhead. That sound wasn't just canvas...it was authority, the kind you could feel in your chest. A flag like that in Shanghai wasn't decoration. It was teeth.

A petty officer barely bothered with my papers. Flicked a glance, jerked a thumb down. "Galley's waiting. Chief'll square you."

The galley slapped me first with steam. Martinez was already there…short, thick, his arms corded tight from years wielding knives. He was chopping onions so fast it sounded like a typewriter hammer on metal. The air stung, and made tears stream before I blinked. A firebox groaned in the corner; the place felt like a furnace.

I stiffened upright. "Franklin M. Hoeffer, Mess Cook, reporting for duty, Chief."

The knife froze mid cut. He raised his head slow.

"How many eggs you scramble yesterday, Hoeffer?"

Mouth stuck up dry. "None, Chief. We were on box lunches during…"

"Wrong." Knife slammed the board, sharp as a gunshot. "Seven hundred. That's breakfast for this crew. Tomorrow you'll beat that number by oh five thirty. Hot. Not cold. Not rubber. Hot. You foul it, every man will know. I'll know."

"Yes, Chief."

"Wash." He didn't blink. "You're already late."

That was my welcome. By night my knuckles burned. Thirty pounds potatoes peeled, boiled, mashed one fork at a time…arm shuddering, sweat running salt down my chin. Martinez scooped, chewed slow, spat into a rag.

"Too bland. Too dry. But serviceable. Carry it out."

The mess deck was a furnace that turned louder. Sweat, grease, smoke stacked thick in the air, men hunched near their trays. Every head turned as I dragged that pan in. Steel forks hitting metal plates like a firing line.

Kelly looked first. Big jaw, scar ran white from lip to chin. Chewing on a cork dry cigar, he grinned through the stub. "Not bad, kid. You'll do."

Later, after pans had been scrubbed raw, Martinez shoved a mug into my hands. Coffee black, bitter, scorched halfway to tar. Scalded my throat straight down. We leaned into the fantail rail. Sampans drifted by, their lanterns bobbing dim reflections. Coal smoke sat heavy and sour.

"You did all right," Martinez said cool, words burned rough. "But all right in this city gets you buried. Shanghai's rotten. The Japs bite closer each week. Only thing that keeps their claws back is that flag. So remember…cook like your life depends on it. Because it does."

I took another swallow, throat on fire, and said nothing.

That pattern set in. Four bells, pots already boiling, coffee perking black and mean. Eggs powdered, foamed into sludge, salted heavy to trick a tongue. Beans burping low on the range. Steam sweating down the steel. And the sailors stumbled through with mugs like lifelines to their lips.

You learned men like that. Plates don't lie. Kelly chewed slow, scar twitching with the bite. "Eat like midnight already has your name." Patterson, cigarette bobbing in unlit lips, hands shaking near constant. Voice low, almost a whisper. "Japan's already won. Steel, air, and will. We're just keeping tally." Thompson plowed through second helpings, laughing loud, grease streaked like armor down his arms. Fork waved wild. "Doesn't matter what busts, I'll put her right. Spit and steel, I'll weld her back myself."

Even Morrison…Captain. Came through once, face lean, eyes cold as the river. He ate slow, set fork flat, and fixed me. "Hoeffer, this roast could serve in San Francisco."

I stammered Martinez's name, but Morrison cut me clean. "Chief gave you bones. You put flesh on. Remember that. A cook holds his crew when nothing else can." Boots rang off into the steel.

Shanghai liberty was no break. The streets slapped worse than the galley. Smell of garlic fried black, fish rotten in the gutter, sweat layers backed with piss. Stalls pressed shoulder to back, voices high and sharp. I thought I could haggle. Bok choy. My tones came wrong. Old woman's eyes bright. Crowd laughing loud, doubling the price every word. She shoved greens into my chest like victory. "Foreign devil pays too much!"

Back aboard, Martinez fried them with garlic. He sniffed. "Paid too much." But his lip tilted, almost a smile.

Ah Ting was different. Officers' cook. Solid, heavy, quiet. He stepped in one night with a neat cloth, laid spinach down.

"For you."

I reached for coin. He waved it away, tight.

"Family safe?" I asked, half stupid.

His jaw locked. "Nanking. Letters until Christmas '37. After... nothing." He folded cloth slow, corners exact like funeral duty. "Maybe gone. Maybe mercy."

He turned before I breathed. I cooked it gentle, butter foaming, garlic spitting. Ate it down while grief rode heavy.

By '39 the city choked full. Refugees stacked in alleys, skin shut over bone, flies rising from sores in black clouds. Mothers held babies to empty breasts, the sound of crying flat with no breath left. Clubs still pumped jazz...bright and frantic. Men blew hard but the notes broke. Japanese troops stood watch, rifles gleaming, faces still.

Then came the *Panay* men. Survivors hauled aboard, oil blackened, burns red raw, uniforms fused to skin. Stench thick...diesel, flesh, smoke. Martinez bellowed. "Coffee, boy!"

I carried the mugs. One lieutenant shook so hard he spilled scalding brown across his hand. His nails clawed my wrist, eyes blood whites turned raw. "They saw us...flags broad as barns. Circled back. Strafed again. Not mistake."

His voice cracked. "Safe? Kid, there's no safe. Not here. Not anywhere."

After that we patrolled upriver under shadows. Japanese ships tailing starboard. Their men saluted tidy. Their guns stayed locked.

Martinez slipped away by '40. Gout swelling him mean. He pressed galley keys into my palm. "Your galley now, Hoeffer. Forty mouths, three meals, every day. Feed them or they fall."

"Yes, Chief."

He turned in the hatch, pain twisting him. "Don't be me. Be better."

From then, galley was mine. Steel scrubbed white, knives lined, tins weighed by ear. Feeding them was my war.

Men laughed. "World ends, Hoeffer's still plating chow." Laughs half joke, half hope. Steam let their shoulders loosen.

Kelly found me one evening in '40, leaning over the stern rail watching the river traffic. "You've been aboard three weeks straight, Hoeffer. Come ashore."

I didn't have an argument against it.

Shanghai at night was a different city than Shanghai in daylight. The checkpoints were still there, the Japanese soldiers still rigid at their posts, but the neon had come on and the streets pulled you forward. Kelly knew where to go—a basement club off the Rue Cardinal Mercier, down a flight of stairs slicked with spilled beer, where a Filipino band was playing something that had started as a fox trot and become something else entirely.

"How do they even know this place exists?" I asked.

"They're Filipino. They know every club in Asia." Kelly flagged down a waiter. "Two Tsingtaos. Don't give me that look, it's better than the Stateside stuff."

He was right. We sat with our bottles and watched the room. British officers. French businessmen. White Russian women who had nowhere left to go. Chinese in Western suits, smoking with the practiced ease of men who'd learned to look comfortable anywhere. Japanese officers at a corner table, watching everything, pretending not to.

"You notice they never dance?" Kelly said.

"Who?"

"The Japanese. They come in, they drink, they watch. Never dance." He took a pull. "Like they're memorizing the place."

The band played on. A trumpet player closed his eyes and went somewhere private with a slow melody, something melancholy enough that even the Japanese officers stopped talking for a moment.

"Martinez says we'll be gone by spring," I said.

"Martinez is usually right." Kelly scraped at the label on his bottle. "You know what I keep thinking about? My mother's kitchen in Akron. Linoleum floor, yellow. Smelled like coffee cake every Sunday morning." He looked at the trumpet player. "Funny what you miss."

"What do you think it'll be like? Manila."

He thought about it. "Hotter. Wetter. More of the same, probably." He finished his beer. "Come on. Let's get another round before they close this place down too."

On the walk back to the ship, we passed an alley where a family of refugees had made camp—a man, a woman, two small children—their entire life piled around them in baskets and bundles. The children were asleep. The man and woman sat awake, very still, watching the street with eyes that had learned not to expect anything.

Kelly reached into his pocket and put some coins on the edge of their blanket without stopping.

We didn't say anything for the rest of the walk back.

By '41 Shanghai was a cage. Checkpoints stiff, rifles fixed. Refugees flooding roads. Morrison bent over maps at all hours, eyes sunk deep. Shore leave dead. Dread in every hand.

Still, I cooked. Spam fried till it crooned ham. Powdered eggs drowned heavy with milk, coffee so thin it turned clear...but hot. Hot mattered.

Kelly smoked beside me one night, scar twitching. Wind stank of coal and dead fish. "Think about what's next, Frank?"

"Every damn day."

"And?"

Smoke burned my throat. "As long as I put plates down, I matter. After that... who the hell knows."

He tipped ash. "Orders are coming. They'll cut deep."

Orders landed November '41: out in seventy-two hours. Destination was Manila.

Chaos bled. Martinez limped cussing, cane rattling metal. Thompson buried in engines, grease dripping. I baked bread until steam filled the ship, roasted every cut worth chewing. Men hunched over heavy trays, voices strangled down.

Ah Ting came last. Pouch tied red. Pressed it into my hand. "Ginger. For cold seas."

At dawn the *Oahu* drew herself loose. Bund shrank small, swallowed behind coal haze. Three years cooked into me vanished in smoke.

| 4 |

Orders to Evacuate

November 1941. Orders came down from Shanghai: all Navy ships and personnel out, destination unknown. War was coming and we were pulling back before it started.

We all thought we might be going to Australia. Nobody wanted to believe we'd end up in the Philippines.

I was in the galley when I first heard. Two seamen stood just outside the hatch, voices low but urgent.

"Evacuation. All personnel. Shanghai's done."

"Where to?"

"Nobody's saying. Scuttlebutt says Australia."

"Australia my ass. We're headed straight into it. Philippines, mark me."

The second voice had it right, though none of us wanted to believe it. Australia was sunshine, distance, safety. The Philippines was different. That name sat heavy in the gut, a weight that pressed down and wouldn't lift.

But underneath it all, you could feel the change. Shanghai was holding its breath.

The orders came official by mid-morning: strip the warehouses, load everything, leave nothing behind. Every available hand to the docks.

We moved fast.

The docks were chaos. Chinese dockworkers swarmed, shouting orders in rapid-fire Mandarin and broken English. American sailors hauled cargo, their uniforms already dark with sweat despite the November chill. Officers barked commands.

I worked alongside the crew, hauling and stacking. My hands were already raw, blisters forming on my palms where the rough wood bit into skin. Sweat ran down my face, stinging my eyes, dripping off my chin.

"Keep it moving!" an officer shouted from the gangway. "We don't have all day!"

Nobody had the breath to answer. We just kept moving, one crate after another, shoulders burning, backs screaming, legs turning to rubber beneath us.

Salt pork barrels came next, and those were the worst. They leaked brine, slick and sticky, leaving trails across the gangplanks that made your boots slip. We lost one barrel that way—it got away from a sailor named Jenkins, rolled straight off the edge and hit the river with a splash that sent brown water across the dock. Jenkins stood there staring at the spot where it disappeared until a chief grabbed him by the shoulder and shoved him back to work.

One man, a kid named Garcia, lost his grip on a crate and it slammed into his shin. The crack was audible even over the noise of the docks. He went down hard, face white with pain, but he was back on his feet in seconds, limping but still working.

By noon, the deck was chaos. Crates stacked high, lashed down with rope. Mailbags bulging with letters—love letters, Dear John letters, letters that probably wouldn't reach home in time. Boxes marked "Consul Records." Personal baggage from American nationals, battered suitcases and trunks that smelled of mothballs and old leather.

The American civilians clustered near the gangway, watching their belongings loaded aboard. They looked lost, displaced, their faces tight with worry and exhaustion. Some of the women held children, trying to keep them calm in the chaos. One little girl clutched a doll, its porcelain face cracked, one eye missing. She stared at the ship with wide, frightened eyes. I wondered what she understood about what was happening.

One man, a businessman in a rumpled suit that had probably been expensive once, stood at the gangway pleading about his horse—a beautiful white animal, reined up by a Filipino stable hand, swatting flies with its tail.

"Please, Captain. I've had him for ten years. He's family. I can't just leave him."

The captain cut him off, voice flat and final, no room for argument. "Not on your life. I'm ordered to carry personnel, families, mail, and baggage. No animals except dogs. That is no dog."

The man's shoulders sagged. The horse was led away, hooves clopping hollow against the stone dock, and the man stood there watching until it disappeared into the crowd.

I kept my focus on the food. That was my job, my responsibility. Every sack of beans, every barrel of pork, every crate of hardtack—it all mattered.

I was responsible for keeping them fed, no matter what happened.

I moved through the galley, checking stores as they came aboard, running my hands over every crate and barrel. Salted fish, their sharp brine smell cutting through everything else. Hardtack, dry and tasteless but vital. Coffee beans. I did the math in my head: so many men, so many days, so much food. Stretch the pork, ration the coffee, make the beans last.

Pitts Eberhardt worked beside me, hauling sacks and crates—my buddy since we'd both come aboard two years ago.

"Feels like we're loading the whole damn city," Pitts grunted, hefting a sack of rice onto his shoulder. "And all of it smells like pig fat and misery."

I laughed, short and sharp. "Better pig fat than nothing."

"True enough." He dropped the sack with a thud that shook the deck and wiped his forehead with his sleeve, leaving a streak of flour across his face. "You think we're really headed for Australia?"

"No."

"Yeah. Me neither." He was quiet for a moment, staring out at the river, at the chaos of the docks, at the city we were leaving behind. "Philippines?"

"Probably."

"Shit."

We didn't say more. Didn't need to. The word hung between us, heavy with everything it implied.

The ship's engines rumbled to life in the early afternoon, a deep thrum that vibrated through the deck and up into my chest. Something irreversible beginning.

The mooring lines cast off, splashing into the muddy water. The anchor windlass groaned, hauling chain link by link—the sound of leaving, the sound of no return.

The boatswain's whistle shrilled. "Sea Detail!"

From the docks, the Chinese shouted their farewells. Some waved. Others stood silent, faces impassive, watching us go with dark, unreadable eyes. A few spat.

The trim white gunboat steamed into the middle of the stream. The anchor was dropped preparatory to turning the ship around and sailing for our first port of call.

Then came the missionaries.

They stood waiting on the dock, a small group in worn, practical clothes—faded cotton dresses, patched trousers, shoes that had been resoled more than once. Their faces were lined, weathered by years in the Chinese sun. But their eyes held a quiet, unshakable conviction, a certainty that bordered on stubbornness.

We offered them passage. Space was tight, the ship already overloaded with cargo and civilians, but we weren't about to leave Americans behind if they wanted out. The captain made it clear—anyone who wanted to go could go.

The woman who spoke for them was older, her hair gray and pulled back tight in a bun. "Our work is here. God will protect us."

A thin man with wire-rimmed spectacles nodded. "They thought the Japanese wouldn't touch them. They were wrong."

We left crates of medical supplies stacked at their feet. Quinine, sulfa drugs, morphine, bandages, iodine. Everything we could spare.

The old woman took a tin of canned milk from one of the crates, her hands trembling. "God bless you, boys," she whispered, her voice cracking. "We will pray for your safe return."

Her eyes were wet, but she didn't cry. She just stood there, holding that tin of milk like it was something precious, something sacred.

As we pulled away, they grew smaller and smaller, until they were just specks against the muddy bank, the crates piled around them like monuments to faith and stubbornness. I watched until I couldn't see them anymore.

Then came the hardest part.

We left the *USS Wake* behind—skeleton crew only, just enough to maintain radio contact.

We never saw those men again.

The Wake sat low in the water, her flag hanging limp in the still air. She was smaller than the *Oahu*, older, her paint more faded, her lines less clean. But she was still Navy, still ours.

I knew men on that ship. A mess cook named Cross, who'd shared cigarettes with me on shore leave, leaning against a wet Shanghai wall, talking about home and girls and what we'd do when we got out, making plans that would never happen. A deckhand they called Red, with a shock of bright red hair and a laugh that could fill a room, who always had a joke ready, who could make you smile even on the worst days, who'd once made me laugh so hard I'd spit coffee across the mess deck.

They stood on her deck as we steamed past, small figures waving, their movements slow and deliberate, like men underwater. One cupped his hands to his mouth and shouted, "See you when you get back!"

His voice was thin, reedy, swallowed almost immediately by the churn of our propellers and the slap of water against the hull. The words reached us, but barely, like an echo from a great distance.

Red just stood there, a cigarette burning down between his fingers, the smoke rising straight up in the still air. He didn't wave. He didn't shout. He just looked at us as we pulled away.

Forty Chinese laundrymen. A handful of Americans. They were still there on December 8 when the world exploded. Prisoners before we even knew we were at war.

The river banks slid past. Small villages, smoke rising from cooking fires, water buffalo in the shallows. Children waved from the banks. Some of the older ones threw stones—not hard enough to reach the ship, but the gesture was clear enough.

The air grew colder as we moved south, the damp chill seeping through uniforms.

At night the river turned black. Mosquitoes descended in clouds, their whine constant, their stings raising welts on every inch of exposed skin.

Cigarettes glowed red in the darkness, scattered across the deck like fireflies.

One night, a sailor standing watch near the galley spoke into the darkness. "You hear the Japs already moved on Manila?"

Nobody answered at first. Then another voice, bitter and tired: "Doesn't matter where they are. We'll see them soon enough."

The talk died there.

The ship turned, her bow cutting clean through the muddy water. Salt touched the air, faint at first, then stronger as we neared the river mouth.

Men kept to their duties. Swabbers dragged wet mops across deck plates. Gun crews ran dry drills, breech open, breech closed, load, unload.

I stayed in the galley, checking stores, stirring pots, stretching every ounce of provisions as far as it would go. Salt pork, beans, coffee rations stretched thin into the bitterest brew I'd ever poured, weak and watery but hot. Hot was hot, and men lifted those mugs like they were gold, like they were the last good thing in the world.

The last sight of inland China slid behind us—huts sinking flat into the banks, smokestacks shrinking to thin pencil marks against the gray sky.

The *Oahu* churned forward, her bow lifting in the stronger pull of the sea, the motion changing from the steady glide of river travel to the rise and fall of ocean swells. Spray cut across the deck, a cold slap to the face.

Shanghai was gone. Wuhu was gone. The missionaries, standing on docks with their crates stacked like gravestones, gone. The Wake's men waving, cigarette smoke curling in cold air, gone.

The Yangtze fell away behind us, and ahead lay only the open sea, gray and endless, and whatever hell waited beyond the horizon.

Storm Passage

November 29, 1941 at 1700 the gunboats, *USS Oahu* and *USS Luzon*, left Yangtze Poo buoys for then unknown destinations. Weather reports had been received telling us that bad weather was to be expected on the trip.

The departure was quiet. No fanfare, no ceremony. Just the low rumble of engines coming to life, the clank of anchor chains, the hiss of steam venting from safety valves. Shanghai fell away behind us, the city lights beginning to glow in the early dusk like dying embers. The Bund's grand buildings stood silhouetted against the gray sky...the Cathay Hotel, the Hong Kong and Shanghai Bank, the Customs House with its clock tower...monuments to an empire that was crumbling. And then they were gone, swallowed by distance and the gathering dark.

I stood on deck for a while, watching China disappear. Two years of my life on that river, two years of knowing every bend and current, every dock and danger, every smell and sound. The Yangtze had been home in a way that no shore posting ever was. Now it was behind us, receding into memory, and ahead lay open water and whatever came next.

Pitts stood beside me, smoking a cigarette cupped in his palm against the wind. He didn't say anything. Neither did I. There wasn't much to say. We both knew we weren't coming back. Shanghai was finished for Americans, the Yangtze Patrol was over, and the life we'd known for years had ended the moment those mooring lines splashed into the muddy water.

"Think we'll see it again?" Pitts finally asked, his voice barely audible over the engine noise.

"No."

He nodded, took a long drag on his cigarette, flicked it over the side. The ember arced through the dusk and disappeared into the wake. "Yeah. Me neither."

Our first two days out were fine, but soon we were to hit the Formosan Straits, which were known to be very rough.

We rounded Formosa and caught a glimpse of the ex-President Hoover, the big American liner, held fast in the jaws of jagged rocks and slowly being lashed to pieces by the pounding waves. The enemy was trying to salvage her but could only work certain times of the year. She sat there getting smaller as we passed, one more thing left behind.

The first two days were almost pleasant, a gift of calm before the storm. The sea was gentle, long swells that lifted the bow and set it down easy, the kind of motion that rocked you to sleep instead of keeping you awake. The sky stayed overcast, a uniform gray that pressed down but didn't threaten. The *Oahu* cut through the water clean, her engines steady, her white hull gleaming even in the dim light. The *Luzon* steamed alongside, her silhouette visible in the distance, rising and falling with the gentle swells like a sister keeping pace.

I kept the galley running smooth. Three meals a day, served hot and on time. Breakfast was oatmeal, coffee, toast when we had bread, bacon when I could manage it without the grease sliding off the griddle. Lunch was sandwiches, soup, more coffee. Dinner was the real meal...meat, potatoes, vegetables from cans, gravy to make it all go down easier. The crew ate well those first two days, and I made sure of it. Good food, hot coffee, full bellies. It was the last normal cooking I'd do for a long time.

The crew settled into the rhythm of open ocean. Four hours on, eight hours off, the routine as familiar as breathing. The air changed as we moved south—warmer, heavier, smelling of open water instead of the coal smoke and river mud of Shanghai. At night the sea was dark and the sky was full of stars and you could almost forget what was waiting at the other end. Men wrote letters in the berthing spaces, their heads bent over paper, trying to find words that were true but not frightening. Others slept the easy sleep of men who hadn't yet remembered what was coming.

But everyone knew what was coming. The Formosan Straits had a reputation that preceded them like a curse. Every sailor who'd been through them had stories...ships rolled nearly on their beam ends, gear torn loose and washed overboard, men swept off decks and never seen again. The straits funneled the weather, concentrated it, turned ordinary storms into something that could break a ship in half. And we were heading straight into them in a river gunboat with a thin hull and low freeboard, a ship never designed for open ocean.

On the third day, the sky changed. The overcast thickened, turned darker, pressing down like a physical weight. The gray went from light to dark to nearly black, and the air took on a strange quality...heavy, oppressive, hard to breathe. The wind picked up, coming in gusts that made the rigging sing and whistle, a high-pitched sound that set teeth on edge. The swells grew longer, deeper, lifting the bow high and dropping it with a shudder that ran through the entire hull, deck plates rattling, rivets creaking.

The barometer was falling. I heard the officer of the deck mention it to the captain, their voices low and tense. Falling fast, he said. Storm coming, and a big one.

By evening of the third day, we were in it.

The storm hit like a fist to the face, sudden and brutal. One moment we were riding heavy swells, the ship pitching but manageable, the next the wind was screaming, and the sea was trying to tear us apart. Rain came horizontally, driven by wind that felt like it could strip paint off steel, each drop hitting like a tiny bullet. Waves crashed over the bow, solid green water that thundered across the deck and drained through the scuppers in white foam that glowed phosphorescent in the dark.

The ship began to roll. Not the gentle rocking of the first two days, but deep, violent rolls that lifted one rail high while the other dipped toward the water, the deck tilting at angles that made walking impossible. You had to hold on, grab for anything bolted down, move hand over hand like climbing a ladder that kept shifting beneath you.

Word was passed to go over all gear and to secure it.

The boatswain's whistle shrilled through the storm, barely audible over the wind. "All hands! Secure for heavy weather! All hands!"

I moved through the galley, lashing down everything that could move. Pots secured with rope, tied to their hooks with extra line. Utensils stowed in lockers, the doors wedged shut with wooden blocks. The big coffee urn tied to its mount with rope thick as my thumb, wrapped around and around until it couldn't budge. Every loose item was a weapon when the ship rolled. I'd seen a cast iron skillet break a man's arm once in heavy weather, flying across a galley like a cannonball, and I wasn't about to let that happen on my watch.

The crew worked fast, moving through the ship with practiced efficiency. Hatches dogged down tight, the wheel spun until the dogs bit into their seats, sealing the openings against the sea. Lifelines rigged on deck, rope strung from bow to stern so men could clip on and not get washed overboard. Anything topside that could be moved was brought below...tools, spare gear, anything not welded or bolted down. The deck gang worked in the driving rain, their oilskins streaming water, boots slipping on wet steel, hands raw from handling cold rope and colder metal.

The *Oahu* wasn't built for this. She was a river gunboat, designed for the Yangtze's muddy water, not the deep Pacific swells. Her hull was thin, her plates light to keep her draft shallow for river work. Her freeboard was low, barely six feet from waterline to deck, which meant every wave that hit came aboard. In heavy seas she felt fragile, like she might come apart at the seams, like the rivets might pop and the plates peel back and the whole ship fold in on itself.

You could hear her straining. The hull plates groaned with every roll, a deep metallic sound that vibrated through your bones. The rivets creaked, thousands of them holding the ship together, each one stressed beyond what it was designed for. The frame members flexed, steel bending in ways steel shouldn't bend. It sounded like the ship was crying, like she was begging to be let out of this hell.

The rolling started that night and never stopped. Long, deep rolls that lifted one rail high while the other dipped toward the water, the deck tilting thirty degrees, forty degrees, more. You could feel the ship straining at the top of each roll, hanging there for a moment that stretched into eternity, and you'd wonder if this was the one, if this was the roll she wouldn't come back from. Then she'd start back, slow at first, then faster, rolling to the other side, and the whole process would repeat.

Everything not secured slid and crashed. In the berthing spaces, men's seabags broke loose and tumbled across the deck, spilling clothes and personal items. Lockers flew open despite being latched, their contents scattering. In the galley, despite all my preparations, things came loose. A pot broke free and clanged across the deck. A drawer full of utensils spilled, knives and forks and spoons sliding back and forth with each roll, making a sound like wind chimes in hell.

Men grabbed for handholds, braced themselves in doorways, wedged themselves into corners. The metal was cold and wet and your palms kept slipping. Moving through the ship became an exercise in timing—wait for the roll, move during the brief moment of level, grab the next handhold before the ship heeled over again. Salt spray came over the bow and found you no matter where you stood. Your clothes were never dry. Nothing was ever dry. Some men gave up and just stayed where they were, holding on, riding it out.

I tried to cook.

Forty-seven degrees. That's not a roll...that's nearly capsizing. When a ship goes past forty-five degrees, you start wondering if she'll come back up. The laws of physics say she should, that the weight of the keel will pull her upright, but physics is just theory when you're hanging onto a bulkhead that's become a floor and water is pouring in through vents that are now below the waterline.

The deck tilts so steep you can't stand, can't walk, can barely hold on. Your feet are on the bulkhead, your hands are gripping what used to be overhead pipes, and everything loose is flying through the air or sliding down what used to be the deck. Water pours in through vents and hatches that can't be sealed tight enough. The world turns sideways and stays there, hanging, while you wait to see if physics will let you live or if this is the moment the ship gives up and rolls all the way over.

The first big roll caught me in the galley with a pan of hot grease on the stove. I was trying to fry meat for the crew's dinner, holding onto the overhead with one hand while managing the pan with the other. It was stupid, dangerous, but the men needed to eat and I was determined to feed them properly despite the storm.

The ship rolled to starboard, slow and ponderous, and kept rolling. The grease tilted in the pan, started to pour over the edge. I grabbed for it with my free hand, but the ship rolled further and the grease went everywhere...across the stove, onto the deck, splashing hot against the bulkhead. Some of it hit my hand, my wrist, burning through skin in an instant.

"Son of a bitch!" I grabbed the pan and shoved it into the sink, grease and all, the hot fat hissing as it hit the wet metal. My hand was burned where the grease had splashed, the skin already blistering, but there was no time to think about it. The ship rolled back to port, just as steep, and everything that had slid starboard now slid back.

Pots clanged against their lashings. Utensils clattered in their drawers. And somewhere below I heard the crash of something heavy breaking loose, followed by shouting.

I gave up on frying. It was suicide. Switched to the ovens instead, figuring roasted meat was safer than boiling grease. Got several pans loaded with meat and into the ovens, then had to hold on as the ship rolled again. The oven doors weren't secured...couldn't be, you needed to check the meat, needed to be able to get at it...and every time we rolled hard the doors flew open with a crash that echoed through the galley.

I developed a rhythm born of desperation. Hang from the over-head with one hand, feet braced against the stove, time the rolls. When the ship heeled to starboard, the port-side oven doors would fly open and the pans would start to slide. Grab the doors, shove the pans back in, slam the doors shut. When the ship rolled to port, the starboard-side oven doors would fly open and the whole process re-peated. Back and forth, over and over, my burned hand screaming every time I grabbed hot metal, my arms shaking with exhaustion, but the meat had to cook and the pans had to stay in the ovens.

The soup pot was worse...a big copper kettle full of hot broth that sloshed and spilled with every roll. I'd tied it down with rope, lashed it to the stove, but the liquid inside had its own momentum. It climbed the sides of the pot with each roll, spilled over the rim, ran across the stove and onto the deck where it mixed with seawater that was leak-ing in from somewhere above. The galley deck became a skating rink of soup and seawater and spilled grease, every step treacherous, every movement a calculated risk.

The galley was a disaster. Water on the deck, ankle-deep in places, sloshing back and forth with each roll. Grease splattered every-where...on the bulkheads, on the overhead, on my clothes and in my hair. Soup and seawater mixing in a slick that made every step treach-erous. My hands were burned, my clothes soaked through, and I was exhausted from fighting the ship's motion, from fighting gravity it-self. But the crew still needed to eat.

Somehow I managed to get the crew's supper out that evening.

I don't know how. Sheer stubbornness, maybe. Or the knowledge that hungry men in a storm are dangerous men, that a crew that isn't fed is a crew that falls apart. I got the meat out of the ovens, somehow kept it in the pans despite the rolling, ladled soup that was more water than broth into cups that men had to hold with both hands to keep from spilling. The crew ate standing up, braced in doorways and against bulkheads, wedged into corners, shoveling food into their mouths between rolls, swallowing fast before the next roll sent everything flying.

Nobody complained. They were too tired, too focused on just staying upright, on keeping the food down. Some of them looked green, seasick despite years at sea. The motion was that bad...violent, unpredictable, the kind of rolling that turned your stomach inside out and made you wish you were dead.

After consulting with the Acting Commissary Steward and Commissary Officer, we decided to have sandwiches and coffee hereafter.

The officer found me in the galley around midnight, both of us holding onto whatever we could reach while the ship tried to shake us loose. He was pale, his uniform soaked, his eyes red from salt spray and exhaustion. Water dripped from his cap, ran down his face, and he didn't bother to wipe it away.

"Can you keep cooking hot meals?" he shouted over the roar of wind and water and the groan of the ship's hull.

I looked at the wreckage of my galley, at the grease and water and spilled soup, at the oven doors that kept flying open, at my burned hands that were blistered and raw. I looked at the stove that was trying to kill me, at the deck that was more ice rink than floor, at the overhead I'd been hanging from for hours.

"Not safely, sir."

He nodded, understanding immediately. "Sandwiches and coffee. Cold food. Whatever you can manage without fire."

"Aye, sir."

It was the right call. Better cold sandwiches than men burned by flying grease or scalded by spilled soup. Better cold food than no food at all because the cook was dead or injured.

I broke out bread, cold meat, whatever I could slap together that didn't require cooking. The bread was stale, the meat was cold and greasy, but it was food. The coffee I kept going...men needed something hot, something to hold onto that felt normal, something that said we were still civilized despite the storm trying to kill us. I lashed the coffee urn down with extra line, wrapped it until it couldn't possibly move, and prayed it would hold.

After several hours of wild pitching and rolling, the forward hold, anchor windlass and forward crew compartments were flooded.

The word came down through the ship like a death sentence, passed from man to man in shouts that barely carried over the storm: "Forward compartments flooding! Forward compartments taking water!"

Water was coming in. Not spray, not leaks around hatches, not the normal seepage you expected in heavy weather. Real water. Green seawater pouring in through hatches and vents that couldn't be sealed tight enough against the waves that kept crashing over the bow. The forward crew quarters were taking it worst, water sloshing ankle-deep, then knee-deep, rising with every wave that broke over the deck.

The pumps were running full out, their motors screaming, but they couldn't keep up. For every gallon they pumped out, two more came in. The ship was taking on weight forward, her bow settling deeper, which meant more water came aboard with each wave, which meant more flooding, a vicious cycle that could only end one way.

Word was passed to abandon the forward crew's quarters and office. The compartments had watertight doors, and after the occupants of the holds had left, they were securely dogged down.

Men came stumbling aft, carrying what they could...seabags slung over shoulders, personal gear clutched in arms, photographs and letters from home stuffed inside shirts to keep them dry. Everything soaked, everything dripping. Their eyes were wide, movements jerky, hands grabbing at anything fixed. Losing the forward compartments meant the ship was in real trouble. It meant we were taking on water faster than the pumps could handle it. It meant we might not make it.

They crowded into the remaining berthing spaces, men packed in tight where there was already no room. No space to lie down, barely room to sit. They wedged themselves wherever they could find a spot, backs against bulkheads, legs drawn up, holding onto their soaked belongings. The air was thick with the smell of wet wool, sweat, vomit from the seasick, and the ever-present stench of bilge water. The ship rolled and rolled, and men held on and prayed and tried not to think about drowning.

I kept making sandwiches. Kept the coffee going. It was all I could do. Feed them. Keep them going. Give them something to hold onto besides fear. Cold meat between stale bread, handed out to men who ate mechanically, not tasting, just chewing and swallowing because their bodies needed fuel. Coffee poured into cups, hot and bitter and strong, something to wrap cold hands around, something to remind them they were still alive.

The storm raged for hours that felt like days. Day turned to night turned to day again and the rolling never stopped. Everything was wet—your clothes, your bunk, the walls. The cold got into your hands until you couldn't feel whether you were holding on or not. The ship smelled of vomit and salt and diesel and the sour fear-sweat of men who'd stopped pretending they weren't afraid. Sleep was impossible. You wedged yourself into a corner and held on, jerking awake when the ship heeled and your gut told you this was the roll it wouldn't come back from.

Topside, gear was tearing loose despite all the securing. The davits that held the small boats were twisted, bent by waves that hit like sledgehammers. Ventilators were smashed flat, crushed by green water. Railings torn away, ripped from their mounts and washed overboard. The ship was being stripped, piece by piece, by a sea that wanted to kill us.

While in these stretches of water, we ran across a Japanese Task Force who quickly surrounded us and wanted to know by radio who we were, our destination, and what port we hailed from.

The storm was still raging when the lookout spotted them. Ships. Lots of ships. Gray shapes in the rain and spray, appearing and disappearing in the heavy seas like ghosts. At first, we thought they might be American, maybe the Asiatic Fleet, maybe help. Then the recognition signals came through, and we knew.

Japanese.

A Japanese destroyer was on our port quarter. It was absurd, for they had all their guns trained on us.

The destroyer came out of the rain like a nightmare made real, her bow cutting through the waves, water streaming off her deck in white sheets. She was bigger than us, faster, newer, built for war. Her guns were manned, crews visible at their stations, barrels trained on our hull, following us as we rolled in the heavy seas. At that range, maybe five hundred yards, she could have blown us out of the water in seconds. One salvo from her main battery would have cut us in half.

Instantly, ours were manned and it was thought a battle would start right there and then.

The alarm sounded, the klaxon cutting through the storm. "General Quarters! General Quarters! All hands man your battle stations!"

Men ran to their stations, slipping on wet decks, grabbing for handholds as the ship rolled, moving with the practiced efficiency of countless drills. The gun crews scrambled to their mounts, training the three-inch guns on the destroyer, loading, ready to fire. It was suicide…we were outgunned, outnumbered, in the middle of a typhoon with our forward compartments flooded…but nobody hesitated. If they were going to sink us, we'd go down fighting. That was the Navy way.

I stood in the galley, holding onto the overhead, watching through the hatch as the destroyer closed. Her guns looked enormous, black holes that could spit death. I could see Japanese sailors on her deck, moving with purpose, efficient and deadly. They wore helmets, life jackets, and they looked ready, eager even.

This was it. My hands had locked on the rail, knuckles gone white, and I couldn't have let go if I'd tried. The cold metal dug into my palms. The spray hit my face so hard it stung like gravel. Not in battle defending something that mattered, not protecting anyone—just a chance encounter in a storm, two ships and the worst possible place and the worst possible time. We'd survived Shanghai. We'd survived the evacuation. We were going to drown in the dark for nothing.

But the Japanese destroyer went past us and everybody breathed easier.

She slid by, close enough that I could see faces on her deck, close enough to read the numbers on her hull, close enough that her wake rolled across ours and added to the chaos of the storm. Her guns stayed trained on us the whole time, following, tracking, ready. And then she was past, disappearing into the rain and spray, her guns no longer pointed at our hearts.

Nobody spoke. We just stood there, holding on, breathing, alive. The relief was physical, a loosening in the chest, a weakness in the legs. Some men sat down right where they were, too shaken to stand. Others laughed, high and nervous, the sound of men who'd just looked death in the face and lived.

They kept coming. Destroyers, cruisers, transports, supply ships, tankers. Twenty vessels, maybe more, all steaming in formation despite the storm, all heading south with purpose. Heading for war. This was an invasion fleet, loaded and ready, moving into position for something big. You could feel it in the way they moved, the discipline, the organization. These weren't ships on patrol. These were ships going to kill.

I watched through binoculars someone handed me, trying to keep them steady as the ship rolled. The vessel was huge, a transport or tender of some kind, her deck crowded with equipment. The davits were massive, far larger than needed for normal ship's boats, heavy steel structures that could lift enormous weight. And suspended in them were strange craft...small, cylindrical, like torpedoes with conning towers. Submarines. One-man submarines, designed to be launched from a mother ship, designed to sneak into harbors and blow themselves up along with their targets. Suicide weapons for a suicide mission.

I had an 8mm movie camera and took pictures of this Japanese Task Force.

My hands shook as I filmed, partly from the cold and exhaustion, partly from the knowledge of what I was seeing. This was intelligence. This was proof of Japanese intentions, proof of their strength, proof that war was coming and coming soon. If we made it to Manila, if we survived this storm and this encounter, these pictures might matter. Might help someone, somewhere, understand what we were facing.

I filmed until the task force disappeared into the storm, until the last gray shape vanished into the rain. Then I secured the camera in my locker, wrapped it in oilcloth to keep it dry, and went back to making sandwiches.

They were going to war. You could see it in every line of every ship...the way they rode low in the water, heavy with fuel and ammunition and supplies. The way their guns were manned and ready. The way they moved with purpose, even in the storm, maintaining formation, maintaining discipline. These weren't ships on patrol or exercise. These were ships going into battle, and soon.

And we were just a small gunboat, alone in a typhoon, watching an empire move to war.

Most of our Chinese native enlisted men (U.S. Navy) were seasick and were sticking close to their bunks, with the exception of Ah Ting, the officer's cook, who was holding up very well.

Ah Ting was a tough old bird, tougher than most of the American crew. He'd been at sea longer than I'd been alive, had weathered storms that would have killed lesser men. While the other Chinese sailors lay in their bunks, groaning and vomiting, too sick to move, Ah Ting kept working. He moved through the officers' galley with the same calm efficiency he always had, making coffee, preparing meals, cleaning up. His face was gray, his hands shook, but he never stopped, never complained.

"You okay, Ah Ting?" I asked during a brief lull, both of us holding onto the galley counter while the ship rolled.

He gave me a thin smile, his weathered face creasing. "Okay, okay. Old man, see many storms. This one bad, but not worst."

"What was worst?"

"Typhoon, 1937. Three days, maybe four. Ship almost sink. Many men die. Water everywhere, ship broken." He shrugged, philosophically. "This storm, we live. Ship strong. Men strong. We live."

I hoped he was right. Prayed he was right.

We rode the rough part of the trip out, pulled into Manila's outer harbor, requested a pilot to escort us in through the heavily mined seaway and dropped anchor opposite Ferry Landing Cavite.

The storm broke on the fourth day. The wind died, the seas calmed, and suddenly we were through. The Formosan Straits were behind us, and ahead lay the Philippines, green and beautiful in the morning sun.

The *Oahu* was a wreck. Her topside gear was gone…davits twisted into abstract sculptures, ventilators smashed flat, railings torn away leaving jagged stumps. The forward compartments were still flooded, water sloshing behind the dogged-down hatches, and it would take days to pump them out. The deck was littered with debris, everything coated in salt and rust. Paint was stripped off in patches, exposing bare metal. But she was afloat. She was moving. She'd survived.

The crew looked worse than the ship. Exhausted, hollow-eyed, moving slow like old men. Some were injured…broken fingers, sprained wrists, one man with a gash on his head from a flying piece of gear that had required stitches. All of us were bruised, battered, worn down to nothing. But we'd made it.

Manila Bay opened before us, wide and calm, the water almost flat after the chaos of the straits. The city was visible in the distance, white buildings gleaming in the sun, palm trees swaying in a gentle breeze. It looked like paradise. It looked like safety. It looked like everything we'd been dreaming of for five days of hell.

We requested a pilot to guide us through the minefields. The harbor was heavily mined, defensive measures against Japanese invasion, rows of mines anchored just below the surface, waiting to blow any ship that strayed from the marked channels. One wrong turn and we'd blow ourselves up after surviving the storm and the Japanese task force. The pilot came aboard, a Filipino in a white uniform, and guided us through the channels marked with buoys, his voice calm and professional as he called out course corrections.

We dropped anchor opposite Ferry Landing Cavite, the anchor chain rattling down, the sound final and absolute. The engines shut down. The vibration that had been constant for five days stopped, and the sudden silence was deafening. Men stood on deck, swaying slightly, their bodies still expecting the roll that didn't come.

The trip took five days and four nights and we had arrived at Manila on December 4, 1941, just three days, seven hours before America and Japan would be at "War".

I stood on that deck, exhausted and burned and grateful to be alive. I'd just cooked my last free meal for nearly four years. I didn't know that yet.

All I knew was that we'd made it. We'd survived the storm, survived the encounter, survived the Formosan Straits. The crew was fed, the ship was afloat, and Manila looked like heaven.

I went below to clean up the galley, to secure the gear properly now that we had time, to prepare for the next meal. Because that's what I did. That's who I was.

| 5 |

Three Days in Paradise

We dropped anchor opposite Ferry Landing, Cavite, on December 4, 1941, just after noon. The trip from Shanghai took five days and four nights, and every man aboard the *USS Oahu* looked like he'd been through a meat grinder. The storm through the Formosan Straits beat us half to death, the Japanese task force scared us worse, and flooding in the forward compartments forced half the crew to sleep in shifts wherever they could find dry space.

But we made it. Manila looked like paradise after Shanghai.

The pilot boat came out to guide us through the heavily mined seaway into the inner harbor. I stood on deck and watched the shoreline sharpen into focus…palm trees swaying in the breeze, white buildings with red tile roofs, the Navy Yard at Cavite sprawling along the waterfront like a small city. Everything looked peaceful. Normal. Like the world wasn't about to catch fire.

"Liberty call at 1700 hours," the word came down from the bridge. "All hands not on watch detail."

The crew let out a cheer that probably carried across the water to Corregidor. We'd been at sea for nearly a week, most of it in conditions that would've killed a normal ship. The *Oahu* was a river gunboat with a thin-plated hull, never meant for the open ocean. That we survived the Formosan Straits at all counted as a minor miracle. The forward hold still flooded, half our topside gear gone, and the galley looked like a bomb had gone off in it. Now we were in port, safe harbor, and the men could finally relax.

I had galley duty until 1600 hours, so I spent the afternoon cleaning up from the voyage. The galley was a disaster...grease splattered on every surface from cooking in those forty-seven-degree rolls, pans dented from being thrown around, the deck still sticky with spilled soup and coffee. Ah Ting, the officers' cook, helped me scrub it down. He was one of the Chinese native enlisted men, U.S. Navy, and he held up better than most during the storm. Never complained, never got seasick, just kept working.

"You think we stay Manila long time?" he asked while we worked, his English careful and precise.

"Don't know," I said, scrubbing at a stubborn grease stain. "Orders said destination unknown. Could be here a week, could be a month."

"Maybe we go Australia."

"Maybe."

I didn't think so. The way those Japanese ships surrounded us in the Formosan Straits, guns trained on us like we were already at war...that didn't look like a navy planning to let us sail peacefully to Australia. Something was coming. We all felt it. You could see it in the way the officers talked in low voices on the bridge, the way the gun crews kept checking their ammunition even though we sat in friendly waters.

By 1700 hours I was cleaned up and ready for liberty. Most of the crew headed into Manila proper...the bars, the restaurants, the girls. I decided to stay closer to Cavite. The Navy Yard had everything a man needed...a decent bar, a restaurant that served real food instead of ship's rations, and a quiet place to walk without the city's chaos.

I went ashore with a couple of other guys from the Yangtze Patrol. We'd served together in China, knew each other's stories, understood what we'd left behind in Shanghai. The missionaries who refused to evacuate. The *USS Wake* with her skeleton crew still sitting at the Yangtze Poo buoys when we pulled out. We didn't talk about it much, but it hung over us like smoke.

The bar near the Navy Yard was called the Bamboo Room, and it was packed with sailors from every ship in the harbor. Gunboats, minesweepers, submarines...everyone who made it out of China or down from the northern Philippines drank San Miguel beer and laughed and pretended the world wasn't falling apart.

"Three days," one of the guys said, nursing his beer. "That's what I heard. Three days and we're moving again."

"Where?" I asked.

"South. Maybe Borneo, maybe Australia. Somewhere the Japs can't reach us."

"The Japs can reach anywhere they want," another guy said. "You saw that task force. Twenty ships, all loaded for war. They're not playing around."

"Yeah, but we're not at war yet," the first guy said. "Maybe it won't come to that."

Nobody believed him, but we let it slide. It was our first night of liberty in weeks, and none of us wanted to spend it talking about war. We drank our beers, told Shanghai stories, and complained about the voyage's food. Normal sailor talk. The kind of conversation that felt like home.

I stayed out until 2300 hours, then caught a water taxi back to the *Oahu.* The harbor lay quiet, just the sound of water lapping against the hulls and the distant hum of generators from the ships. I stood on deck for a while before heading below, looking out at the lights of Manila across the bay. Everything looked so normal. So peaceful. The city glowed against the dark sky, and music drifted across the water from somewhere.

Three days, I thought. We've got three days.

I didn't know they would be my last days of freedom for nearly four years.

Friday, December 5th. The day started like any other peacetime Navy day. Reveille at 0530, breakfast at 0600, then the regular routine of cleaning, maintenance, inventory checks. The crew relaxed, joked around, let the tension from the voyage bleed off. Manila felt safe, insulated, like the war in China sat a thousand miles away instead of across the South China Sea.

I spent the morning in the galley doing inventory. We burned through a lot of supplies on the voyage...flour, coffee, canned goods. I needed to know what we had left and what we needed from Navy Yard stores. Ah Ting helped me count, writing the numbers in his careful hand.

"We need more flour," he said. "Maybe fifty pounds."

"More than that," I said. "We're feeding sixty men three times a day. Better make it a hundred."

"Coffee too. Almost gone."

"Yeah. And sugar. And rice."

The list kept growing. By the time we finished, I had two pages of supplies we needed. I took it to the Commissary Officer, who looked it over and nodded.

"I'll put in the requisition today," he said. "Should have everything by Monday."

Monday. Three days away. It seemed like plenty of time.

That afternoon I went ashore again, this time with a different group. We walked through Cavite...past machine shops and dry docks, past rows of warehouses stacked with supplies. The Navy Yard sprawled like a small city, one of the biggest in the Pacific, and it hummed even on a Friday afternoon. Ships in repair, supplies moving, crews coming and going. Filipino workers everywhere, lifting, welding, painting.

"This place could hold out forever," one guy said. "Look at all this. Food, ammunition, fuel...everything we need."

"Corregidor's even better," another said. "I heard they've got supplies for twenty years. The Japs could throw everything they've got at it and never take it."

I kept quiet, thinking about those Japanese ships in the Formosan Straits. Twenty of them, all heavily loaded, all ready for action. If they planned something big, I didn't think Corregidor's supplies would matter much. You can't eat supplies if you're dead.

We ended up at a small restaurant near the waterfront, the kind that catered to Navy men. The owner, a Filipino who'd worked with the Navy for twenty years, knew how to cook American food. We ordered hamburgers and fries. After weeks of ship's rations, it was the best meal I could remember.

"You think we really go to Australia?" one of the guys asked.

"I don't know," I said. "Maybe."

"I hope so. I got a cousin in Sydney. Be nice to see him."

"I just want to get away from the Japs," another said. "Every time I close my eyes, I see those destroyers with their guns pointed at us."

"We all do," I said.

That night I stayed aboard. The galley needed a deep clean, and I wanted to get ahead on meal prep for the weekend. Ah Ting helped me inventory the stores again…flour, rice, canned goods, coffee. We had enough for maybe two months if we rationed carefully, longer if we resupplied in Manila.

"You think we leave soon?" Ah Ting asked.

"Probably," I said. "Orders could come any day."

"I hope we go south. Away from Japan."

"Yeah. Me too."

Even as I said it, I knew it didn't matter where we went. The war was coming, and we couldn't outrun it. You could see it in the way officers moved, the way they checked and rechecked the guns, the way they studied the horizon like they expected Japanese bombers any minute.

Saturday, December 6th. Another beautiful day in paradise. The sun came up over Manila Bay like it always did, turning the water gold and pink. The air smelled like salt and tropical flowers. Birds sang in the palm trees along the shore.

I served breakfast at 0600…scrambled eggs, bacon, toast, coffee. Real food, not the sandwiches and cold rations we ate during the storm. The crew ate like they were starving, which they probably were after that voyage.

After breakfast I grabbed a few hours and went topside to watch the harbor. Ships everywhere...gunboats, minesweepers, submarines, supply vessels. The *USS Luzon* anchored nearby, her crew working on deck, repairing storm damage. Beyond her, the minesweepers Pigeon and Quail sat at anchor. They met us two hundred miles out and escorted us through the mined seaway.

Corregidor sat in the bay's mouth like a fortress, which is exactly what it was. I could see the big guns on the cliffs, the barracks, the tunnel entrances. It looked impregnable. Unbreakable.

I hoped that was true.

That afternoon I went ashore one more time. A group of us caught a bus from Cavite into Manila proper. The city looked beautiful...palm trees along the boulevards, Spanish colonial buildings with red tile roofs and wrought-iron balconies, the smell of tropical flowers mixing with the bay's salt air. Filipinos everywhere, running Saturday routines. Families shopping, kids playing, street vendors selling fruit and roasted peanuts.

We found a restaurant near the Luneta, the big park along the waterfront. It was a nice place...white tablecloths, ceiling fans, waiters in clean uniforms. We ordered lunch...roasted chicken, rice, fresh vegetables. Real food, not canned goods.

"This is the life," one guy said, leaning back. "I could get used to this."

"Don't get too comfortable," I said. "We'll be back at sea soon enough."

"Maybe. But until then, I'm enjoying every minute."

After lunch we walked the city, stopped at a few shops, watched Filipinos go about their business. Everything felt normal. Safe. Like the war was far away, not crouching on our doorstep.

We passed the Army Navy YMCA, a big building near the waterfront. Sailors and soldiers went in and out, and music played inside. It looked like a good place...a place to relax, write letters home, maybe play cards.

I didn't know that in a few weeks the Japanese would seize it, kick out the secretaries, and steal everything. I didn't know the building I looked at would become enemy headquarters.

We got back to the ship around 1900 hours, just as the sun set over Manila Bay. The water lay calm, reflecting the orange and pink sky. I stood on deck and watched. One of those perfect evenings where everything feels right with the world. The kind you remember later, when everything's gone to hell.

I went below, cleaned up, and turned in early. Tomorrow was Sunday, my last day of liberty. Monday we'd be back to the routine. Galley duty at 0500 hours, breakfast for the crew, then whatever orders came down from the bridge.

I fell asleep grateful to be in Manila instead of Shanghai. We made it through the storm, past the Japanese task force, into safe harbor.

Three days in paradise.

Sunday, December 7, 1941.

I woke at 0530, same as always, but Sunday ran different. No regular work details, just watch duty and meal prep. I served breakfast at 0700...pancakes, bacon, coffee. The crew ate slow, enjoying the lazy Sunday morning.

After breakfast I cleaned up the galley, then got permission to go ashore. A few of us caught a bus from Cavite into Manila around 1000 hours. The city stayed quieter on Sunday...families dressed for church, streets less crowded than Saturday.

We found a small café near the waterfront and ordered coffee. Real coffee, not Navy brew. We sat an hour, watched the city wake, talked about nothing important. Where we'd go if we got leave in Australia. What we'd do when the war ended. Normal peacetime talk.

Around noon we found a restaurant and ordered lunch. I had roasted chicken again with rice and vegetables.

After lunch we walked the Luneta. Families picnicked, kids played, couples walked hand in hand. Everything looked normal. Peaceful. Like the world wasn't about to explode.

We caught a bus back to Cavite around 1600 hours. I wanted to get back early, make sure everything was ready for Monday. The galley needed prep, supplies checked, menus planned.

I got back to the *Oahu* around 1700 hours. The sun started to set, turning the sky orange and gold. I stood on deck a while, watching the light fade over Manila Bay. The water lay calm, like glass, reflecting the sky's colors.

It was beautiful.

I went below around 1900 hours, wrote a quick letter home, then turned in. Tomorrow was Monday, back to work. Galley duty at 0500 hours, breakfast at 0600, then the usual routine.

I fell asleep thinking about the chicken I ate for lunch, about how good it felt to be in port, about how lucky we were.

I didn't know that in a few hours everything would change.

I didn't know I had just spent my last day of freedom for nearly four years.

Monday, December 8, 1941.

I woke at 0445 hours, same as always. The ship lay quiet, just the usual sounds of men sleeping and the gentle creak of the hull against the anchor chain. I dressed in the dark, splashed water on my face from the basin, and headed to the galley.

Ah Ting was already there, starting the coffee. He looked worried, his face tight.

"You hear?" he asked.

"Hear what?"

"Radio. Something happen. Something bad."

Before he could explain, the general alarm sounded. Not a drill...the real thing, the harsh clang that meant battle stations, all hands on deck, now, move move move.

I ran topside with everyone else. The deck turned chaotic...men scrambling to positions half dressed, officers shouting orders, gun crews manning the 3-inch guns and .30-caliber machine guns. The captain stood on the bridge, binoculars on the sky.

"What's happening?" I asked a gunner's mate.

"Pearl Harbor," he said, white-faced. "The Japs bombed Pearl Harbor. We're at war."

The words didn't make sense at first. Pearl Harbor was in Hawaii, thousands of miles away. How could the Japanese have...

"All hands, this is the captain," the loudspeaker crackled. "As of approximately 0600 hours this morning, the United States is at war with Japan. Pearl Harbor Naval Base has been attacked. We are now on wartime status. All liberty is cancelled indefinitely. All guns will remain manned around the clock. Prepare for possible air raids. This is not a drill. I repeat, this is not a drill."

The deck went silent a moment while every man processed it. War. We were at war. The thing we all dreaded, the thing we saw coming since Shanghai, finally landed.

Then someone said, "Those bastards," and the spell broke. Men cursed, checked weapons, scanned the sky.

I went back to the galley in a daze. War. We were at war. I needed to make breakfast, but my hands shook. Ah Ting stood by the stove, staring at nothing.

"War," he said quietly. "We at war now."

"Yeah," I said. "We're at war."

I started breakfast on autopilot...scrambled eggs, bacon, toast, coffee. The crew needed to eat, war or no war. That was my job. Feed the men. Keep them going.

My mind raced. Pearl Harbor bombed. How bad? How many ships? How many men? If they hit Pearl Harbor, they'd hit Manila next. We sat like ducks in the harbor.

I served breakfast at 0630. The crew ate in silence, too shocked to talk. Some looked scared. Some looked angry. All looked like someone yanked the rug from under them.

After breakfast I went topside. The harbor buzzed...ships moving, supplies loading, orders shouted across the water. Everyone prepared for war.

Manila lay across the bay. The city looked the same…palm trees, white buildings, peaceful. But everything changed. We were at war now. The Japanese were coming.

And I would never go ashore again.

The first days blurred…confusion and fear. We stayed at battle stations around the clock, rotating in shifts, always watching for bombers. The harbor churned…ships in and out, supplies moving, orders changing by the hour.

Manila newsboys ran through the streets screaming: "Pearl Harbor bombed! War declared! Philippines next!"

We didn't know what happened to our ships in Hawaii. We didn't know how bad it was. Rumors flew…the entire Pacific Fleet destroyed, thousands dead, Japanese invading California. Nobody knew the truth.

We only knew the Japanese struck first, struck hard, and now we sat in their crosshairs.

I kept the galley running. Three meals a day, every day, no matter what. The crew needed to eat. That was my job. Feed the men. Keep them going.

Supplies tightened fast. The requisition I put in Friday never came…the Navy Yard was too busy. I made do with what we had. Stretched the flour, rationed the coffee, used every scrap.

The air raids started on December 10th.

I was in the galley preparing lunch when the alarm sounded. I dropped everything and ran topside. The northern sky filled with planes…Japanese bombers flying in perfect formation. Twenty-seven in a V, then another twenty-seven, then another. Eighty-one bombers at maybe 15,000 feet, heading straight for Cavite Navy Yard.

"All guns, open fire!" the captain shouted.

Oahu's 3-inch guns roared to life, joined by every ship in the harbor. Black puffs of anti-aircraft fire peppered the sky, but the Japanese flew too high. Our guns couldn't reach them.

The bombs started falling.

I'd never seen anything like it. The Navy Yard erupted in fire and smoke, explosions rippling across docks and warehouses. Buildings collapsed, ships burst into flames, the air filled with screams and the roar of destruction. The ground shook even out in the harbor. Debris rained into the water.

We kept firing, trying to hit anything, but the bombers flew on untouched. They dropped their loads methodically, precisely, turning Cavite into an inferno. I could feel the heat even from our deck.

When they finally left, the Navy Yard was gone. Smoke and fire and rubble. The machine shops where I walked three days ago...gone. The warehouses full of supplies...gone. The restaurant where we ate hamburgers...gone.

Thousands of Filipinos lay dead. Hundreds of American sailors. The USS Sea Lion, a submarine in dry dock, took such damage they scuttled her. The USS Canopus took a 500-pound bomb down her shaft alley, crippling her engines.

And we hadn't shot down a single Japanese plane.

That night I stood in the galley, staring at the pots and pans, trying to figure out how to feed the crew. Half our supplies were gone, destroyed in the bombing. The cold-storage plant at Cavite took a hit; the doors jammed shut with tons of frozen meat trapped inside. The Army bakery near Queen's Tunnel on Corregidor lay in ruins...no more bread.

But the men still needed to eat.

I pulled what I had...rice, canned vegetables, some salt pork. Not much, but enough for a meal. I fired up the stove and cooked, same as always. Rice and vegetables, hot coffee, nothing fancy.

Ah Ting came in, face streaked with soot from fighting fires on deck.

"Bad day," he said quietly.

"Yeah."

"Many people die. Filipinos, Americans. Many die."

"Yeah."

"You think we survive this?"

I didn't answer right away. I kept stirring the pot, watched the rice bubble and steam. The galley smelled like smoke from the fires across the bay. Everything smelled like smoke now.

"We'll survive," I said at last. "We have to."

Even as I said it, I wasn't sure I believed it.

The paradise of three days ago was gone. Manila burned. The Japanese were coming. And I was a ship's cook on a river gunboat with a thin-plated hull, anchored in a harbor that had become a shooting gallery.

I served dinner that night…rice and vegetables, hot coffee, nothing fancy. The men ate in silence, too exhausted and shell-shocked to talk. Some cried. Some stared at their plates. All looked like they aged ten years in one day.

Pitts clutched his tin tray. "This all you got, Frank?"

"What you see," I said. "Rice, vegetables, coffee thin enough to see through."

He sniffed the mug. "Tastes like bilge."

"Drink it anyway. It's hot, keeps your hands warm."

He chewed in silence, then muttered, "Feels like we aged ten years in one day."

"You did," I said. "So did I."

When they finished, they went back to their battle stations, and I went back to the galley to clean up.

Three days, I thought. Three days of walking through Manila, eating real food, feeling safe.

Ah Ting leaned against the bulkhead, face streaked with soot. "Three days ago, I walk in market. Buy oranges. Laugh with girls. Now…" he gestured toward the burning skyline…"all gone."

I kept stirring the pot, steam fogging my face. "Three days," I said.

He nodded slowly. "And now hell."

I said nothing, because he was right.

And now the war had begun.

I looked out the porthole at the fires burning across the bay. Cavite still burned, would burn for days. The sky glowed orange and red. Smoke blotted out the stars.

I thought about the restaurant where I ate chicken on Sunday. The café where we had coffee. The streets where families walked. All of it was probably gone now. Burned. Destroyed.

Three days in paradise.

And then hell came to Manila.

| 6 |

War Begins

The morning of December 8, 1941, Manila newsboys screamed: "Pearl Harbor bombed!"

"Pearl Harbor? You drunk, kid?"

"No, swear to God. Newsboys are screaming it all over Escolta."

"Bull. Hawaii's halfway to America…safe as your mother's kitchen."

"Safe yesterday. Not today. The Japs lit it up this morning."

Silence held for a beat, then Pitts muttered, "If they can hit Hawaii, they'll chew us alive here."

Those of us ashore had no inkling of what happened to our ships. Word came down: we were at war, wartime status. We manned all our guns and stood by for air raids.

"Range fifteen thousand feet, can't see a thing," the gunner grumbled, adjusting his sights.

"Don't need to see 'em. Just fire where the captain says," his loader shot back.

Somebody barked a laugh. "Great. We're a bunch of blind men throwing rocks at the sky."

"Shut it and keep those belts linked," the chief growled. "When they come, they come fast."

I'd been on liberty in Manila the night before. The city pulsed with music and laughter, streets packed with sailors and soldiers who didn't know they were living the last hours of peace. I walked back to the ship just after dawn, my head buzzing from too much San Miguel and not enough sleep. The harbor lay quiet. A few gulls circled overhead. The water sat flat and gray.

Then the newsboys started shouting.

At first, nobody believed it. Pearl Harbor? Hawaii? The Japanese hit us there? It didn't make sense. We were the ones out here in the Pacific, anchored off Cavite, close enough to smell the enemy. Hawaii sat thousands of miles away, safe behind the big guns of the Pacific Fleet.

But the newsboys kept shouting, officers started running, and within minutes the word came down: all hands to battle stations. We scrambled to our posts. The 3-inch guns loaded. The .30-caliber machine guns manned. We scanned the sky, waiting for the first wave of Japanese bombers to scream out of the clouds.

They didn't come that morning. But we knew they would.

After my return Monday morning, December 8, from liberty in Manila, I never went ashore again until the end of the war in the Philippines.

The Japanese navy, with army transports, landed in Lingayen Gulf on December 19, 1941, taking heavy losses but achieving their objective. The invasion had begun. The enemy stood on Philippine soil, and we couldn't stop them.

Soon, we took air raids without counting.

The first big raid came without warning. One moment the sky stood clear, the next it filled with the drone of engines. High above us, in perfect V-formations, Japanese bombers came on. They flew so high we could barely see them...15,000 feet, maybe higher. Our anti-aircraft guns opened up, but the shells burst far below the enemy. The bombers flew on, untouched, and began dropping their bombs.

One day, Japanese dive bombers came in over Manila Harbor and tried to strafe and sink old World War I destroyers...the USS Peary, USS Paul Jones, and USS Pope. After several hours of strafing and bombing, the gallant ships escaped to sea and waited until nightfall to come back to Manila Harbor. They limped in, badly damaged, needing repairs at Cavite Navy Yard.

Every ship around Cavite and Manila threw heavy anti-aircraft fire at the dive-bombers to no effect as the planes climbed into the clouds. That night, the damaged destroyers crept back into port. Crews would repair them quickly, and they'd try to make Australia. To stay in Manila waters would be foolhardy; the Japanese meant to destroy every U.S. warship. Those old fighting-cans later figured big in the Battle of Makassar Strait.

We watched them go. We knew we'd never see them again.

Word reached us later about the H.M.S. Petrol, a small British gunboat that had been hailed by a Japanese cruiser and ordered to surrender. Their answer was a flash of gunfire—a direct hit on the cruiser's bridge. The big Japanese cruiser, over ten thousand tons, opened up with her 8-inch rifles and blew the Petrol out of the water with few survivors. That was how that small gunboat met her end. I thought about it for a long time.

One of the larger Japanese raids sent three flights of twenty-seven bombers each...eighty-one in all. The USS Canopus lay moored alongside Manila's Pier 7 and took many raids. A 500-pound bomb plunged down her shaft alley, wrecking her engines and bending the shaft so badly that, after patching bomb damage, she could only make 6-8 knots at most. That speed made her easy prey for Japanese planes or submarines. The grand old Canopus stayed on to help any U.S. submarines damaged and brought into Manila.

The Cavite yard force and the tenders fought like veterans under terrible conditions, trying to get every craft that could float to other docks not blown up. We lost many old Navy hands in one of the largest raids on Cavite. The bombs killed thousands of Filipinos and many service personnel.

I watched from *Oahu's* deck as the bombs fell. The yard erupted in flames. Huge columns of black smoke rose and blotted out the sun. Concussions rolled across the water like thunder. Men ran, screamed, burned. Filipinos, unprepared for proper cover against bombers, stood in the open, staring at the sky, and the bombs fell on them like rain.

The raids came so large and fast that the Cavite Navy Yard almost ceased to exist. The enemy flew between 15,000 and 23,000 feet and did a thorough job. Fires the bombs started burned for days.

At night, the sky over Cavite glowed red. The smell of burning oil and flesh drifted across the harbor. We stood watch with handkerchiefs tied over our faces, but it didn't help. The stench got into everything…our clothes, our hair, our food.

A few days after the raid, crews from the gunboats and minesweepers salvaged the Commissary store. The bigger ships had left for parts unknown earlier in December 1941.

We scrounged what we could…canned goods, flour, rice. Anything not blown apart or burned. We loaded it onto the *Oahu* and stowed it below. We didn't know how long we'd need it, but we knew we'd need it a long time.

Right after Christmas, high officials decided to abandon Manila and Cavite. The Japanese pressed close to Manila and demanded surrender from U.S. Army headquarters.

Christmas passed strange and quiet. No carols, no decorations. Just distant explosions and the knowledge the enemy was closing in. Some men tried to make the best of it. They sang a few songs, shared what little they had. Most of us sat in silence, thinking about home, the families we'd left, the war that crashed down fast and hard.

After consulting the high command, we declared Manila an open city. Even then, the enemy bombed Manila and killed many Filipinos.

Orders demanded that all guns be surrendered, and civilians were told to offer no armed resistance when Japanese forces entered the city. The U.S. Army had to abandon a large lot of 8-inch rifles and over a million tons of powder and ammunition at Sunset Beach. Destroying that much ammunition would have blown Manila off the map. Moving the huge 8-inch rifles…hundreds of tons each…was impossible; no ship could carry them to Corregidor.

We watched the Army blow what they could and abandon the rest. Bitter work, leaving all that firepower. But we had no choice. The enemy was coming, and we had to fall back.

They said Corregidor held food and ammunition for twenty years. They also said no enemy ships would ever slip past the Fortress of Corregidor, which later proved true. Not one ship entered Manila Harbor until Corregidor surrendered.

By losing Manila, United States Forces Far East forfeited millions in supplies and equipment we could never replace. Wrecked and burning ships studded Manila Harbor and the shores of Cavite and Bataan. United States Forces Far East fell back to Bataan, Corregidor, and other small islands. General MacArthur moved headquarters to Corregidor and from there directed American and Filipino forces against the "Devil Dwarfs" (the Japanese).

We steamed out of Manila Harbor in the early morning, the *Oahu* and the other gunboats moving slowly through wreckage. Burned-out hulks lay half-submerged. Oil slicks spread across the surface, shimmering in the dawn light. The city behind us sat dark and silent.

The Japanese occupied Manila on January 2, 1942. The stories reached us through Filipinos who slipped over to Corregidor. Bayonets in the streets. Women taken. Banks seized, businesses stripped, the peso made worthless overnight. The Jai Alai stadium converted for entertainment, the YMCA gutted. Everything American either destroyed or absorbed. The city we knew, the streets we'd walked on liberty, didn't exist anymore.

American gunboats of the Navy Inshore Patrol...the *USS Luzon*, *USS Oahu*, and *USS Mindanao*...often watched the enemy through powerful night-glasses and noted the big marquee lights blazing and the music carrying clear over the water.

We slipped close to the Manila breakwater at night, darkened ship, engines barely turning over. Through the night-glasses we saw the enemy celebrating. Neon lights blazed. Music drifted across the water. Japanese soldiers staggered through the streets, drunk and laughing. It turned our stomachs.

"Look at them," one of the gunners said. "Living it up while we're out here eating rice and canned beans."

"Don't worry," I said. "Their turn's coming."

But I didn't believe it. Not then.

Every day the former Radio Manila broadcast to Corregidor and played songs aimed at men on Bataan, Corregidor, and other American-held forts. One song was "Waiting for Ships That Never Came In," and captured Filipino soldiers read speeches entreating Corregidor to surrender now or face annihilation.

Day after day, the voice of a Filipino lieutenant told his story about how well the Japanese treated him. We soon learned the lieutenant...with the Filipino Constabulary...wasn't live on air but speaking from a phonograph recording. One day something went haywire, the voice ran down quickly, and they cut the recording. We never heard from the lieutenant again. After that, they played "Waiting for the Ships That Never Came In" often.

We laughed at first. The propaganda was clumsy, obvious. After a while, it stopped being funny. Because the ships really weren't coming. And we all knew it.

Air raids hammered Corregidor, Bataan, and other forts with increasing violence.

The war had begun. Manila had fallen. And we were trapped.

The Japanese air force flew at altitudes from 15,000 to 27,000 feet. Cabcaben, Bataan headquarters and motor pool, took heavy bombings day after day, and the roads from Mariveles and the Bataan front lines broke apart under hits.

We watched bombers come in daily, high silver specks against the blue sky. They flew in perfect formation, untouchable, and dropped bombs with methodical precision. Explosions rolled across the water. Thick black smoke climbed from Bataan. We could only watch.

The U.S.A. airfield at Real Point, about nine miles from Corregidor, also took heavy bombing from 20 to 50 medium bombers. Only five P-40s used this field, never standing in the open, carefully concealed in the sugar-cane fields.

Those five P-40s were all we had left. Five fighters against the entire Japanese air force. But they fought like hell.

Once a P-40 tried to land as Japanese medium bombers unloaded on the field. Great clouds of smoke and dust rose. Observers muttered, "Well, we lost another P-40," but within minutes the lone P-40 appeared, climbing toward Japanese fighters above.

A great cheer went up from the men on *Oahu's* deck. We shouted and waved our hats. The P-40 climbed straight into the formation, guns blazing. Soon the one P-40 dogfought six Japanese fighters. While he mixed it up, four more P-40s joined the furious fight. Before long, the P-40s shot down all the Japanese fighters without losing a single plane.

We watched them fall, trailing smoke and fire, spinning into the sea. It was the only victory we'd seen in weeks, and it felt like a miracle.

A great number of Chinese and Filipinos stayed in a camp at Cabcaben. One day Japanese bombers caught them off guard and killed and wounded many. After that, the rest of the Chinese and Filipino refugees moved to Corregidor for safety.

Filipino scouts played a great role in the fight against the Devil Dwarfs and took a heavy toll.

At 10:00 A.M. on March 27, 1942, a Filipino scout came aboard *Oahu's* fantail to see the ship's cook. He offered to trade twelve little brown ears strung on a wire for food and American cigarettes.

I stared at the ears...dried, leathery, strung like beads. The scout grinned, proud of his trophies.

"You want more?" he said. "I get you more. Easy."

I shook my head. "No thanks."

He shrugged. I declined his offer and traded cigarettes for a bolo and some coconuts. Most of the time Filipino scouts brought back proof of their killings. In a pinch, Filipino scouts fought cool and magnificent.

In the Pukow Hill charge, a naval battalion led by the late Commander Bridget hit a furious battle and about half the men went down wounded under heavy Japanese fire. For a while, the charge nearly broke, but Filipino scouts jumped into the fray and saved the day, driving the enemy into retreat.

Japanese snipers became a constant nuisance, and the naval battalion decided to clear them out. Men took twelve-gauge shotguns and, in staggered positions, walked toward suspected areas. They sprayed the trees and bushes and dropped sixteen Japanese.

The Craig Hill 12-inch howitzers started firing April 4, 1942, just at dusk. They threw shells over at the enemy through the night. Bataan patrols reported that the craters extended a thousand yards. For a while we thought it might make a difference. By then we knew it wouldn't, but you took hope where you found it.

Japanese forces on Bataan kept fresh reinforcements, cold beer, and comforts flowing, while our troops starved and collapsed from exhaustion. Many times supplies intended for front-line troops never arrived, or after we landed stores to be picked up by motor transports, enemy bombers hit the trucks.

Japanese dive-bombers flew over American lines and dropped pamphlets, filthy postcards, and crude drawings supposedly sent by American POWs in Manila, captured when the city surrendered. The cards showed men living well after "royal" treatment by the enemy. The Americans and Filipinos fighting ignored the trash.

Before long, pamphlets rained down on the front lines with English text: "American soldiers, arise...kill your officers...cease fighting and suffering. Give yourself up! Your officers are sacrificing you to preserve their own skins! They care nothing for you. While you are starving, they are gaining weight!"

We picked up one pamphlet that drifted onto *Oahu's* deck. Cheap paper, crude printing. Absurd message. But it reminded us how desperate the enemy was to break our morale.

"Look at this garbage," a gunner said, crumpling the pamphlet and tossing it overboard.

"They think we're stupid," another said.

"They're the stupid ones," I said. "If they think that's going to work."

That propaganda only made our men fight harder.

The Voice of Freedom bolstered us time after time, always opening with: "This is the Voice of Freedom, broadcasting from somewhere in the Philippines." The station broadcast from Malinta Tunnel.

We listened every night. It was our lifeline, our connection to the world outside. The announcer's voice stayed calm, steady, reassuring. He told us help was coming. He told us to hold on. He told us America hadn't forgotten us.

One broadcast announced that 100 ships were on the way from America to help the nearly exhausted troops. Help was on its way at last! Everybody felt good after that, but while on the way, the large force of ships diverted to Australia. The Philippine situation had turned so bad, and Japanese domination of Asia so thorough, that command deemed it futile to sacrifice more men or ships.

We never heard that part on the Voice of Freedom. We learned later, after the surrender. Even then, through those dark days of January, February, and March, we knew. Deep down, we knew the ships weren't coming. We knew we were on our own.

American forces were outnumbered four and a half to one. The Japanese fielded about 250,000; American forces...including Navy, Marines, U.S. Army, plus Filipinos...numbered about 60,000. With no reserves for reinforcement or rest, the American gunboats played a great part in the fight against the Devil Dwarfs.

Sometime in March 1942, Corregidor ordered the gunboats *Mindanao*, *Luzon*, and *USS Oahu* to rendezvous near Real Point, about nine and a half miles from Corregidor. We were to wait for darkness and then, with darkened ships, proceed to Manila and Sangley Point. Our mission: learn what the Japanese were doing and skirt the Bataan shoreline to watch for any forces leaving or entering Bataan.

We slipped out of Corregidor just after sunset, running dark, engines barely turning over. The water lay black and flat. No moon. No stars. Only the engine's thrum and the slap of water on the hull.

About 2200 (10:00 P.M.), the gunboats held about 500 yards off Sangley Point. Through night-glasses we saw no repairs to the damage from Japanese bombs and our own scorched-earth work. Before we abandoned Sangley Point, naval forces destroyed every installation.

Satisfied, Captain Hoeffel of the *USS Mindanao* took us toward the Manila breakwater. Through powerful night-glasses we saw neon lights blazing in various establishments. Japanese Army trucks moved around, but never toward the outer harbor. If they had come out, the gunboats would have opened fire and likely gone down fighting.

Nearly all the crew knew the risk and took it willingly. These men had served on the Yangtze River Patrol in China and knew Japanese tricks, deceptions, and cruelties. They itched for a fight.

We stood at our guns, watching the lights of Manila...the city we knew, the city we loved...now under the enemy's boots. The feeling ran strange and bitter. We wanted to strike back. All we could do was watch and wait.

The war had begun. Manila had fallen. Bataan lay under siege. And Corregidor...the Rock, the fortress that was supposed to hold forever...took a daily pounding into dust.

We didn't know it then, but we had only a few months of freedom left. A few months before the end came, before the white flag went up, before we became prisoners of the Devil Dwarfs.

For now, we fought. We held on. We did our duty.

And we waited for the ships that never came.

| 7 |

The Fighting Cook

The enemy hit us every day with dive-bombers, and we drove them off with our gun crews and Corregidor's guns.

That rhythm set in after the night raid on the Japanese barges. Every morning at dawn, the bombers came. Every afternoon, they came again. And every time they came, I worked the galley to feed the crew.

The klaxon wailed and men pounded past the hatch.

"Frank! Two minutes…anything hot?" Pitts shouted, bracing in the doorway.

"Coffee's boiling. Sandwiches if the stove doesn't try to kill me."

"Save the heroics. Bread's fine."

A loader stumbled in, helmet askew. "You got salt? Mouth tastes like rust."

I slid a shaker across. "Take cups and go. Don't crowd the hatch."

Topside, the first bursts thudded the plates. Dust sifted from the overhead.

Pitts grabbed two mugs. "If we live through noon, I'll come back for seconds."

"You'll take what's left," I said. "Raiders hit the barges again…stores run thin."

He paused, eyes flicking to my crates. "How thin?"

"Count the loaves. That's how thin."

Another blast. The deck jumped.

"See you after," he said.

"Bring my pot back," I told him. "Men fight worse when they're dry."

Fighting in Bataan turned brutal. Our troops bled from dysentery, malaria, and hunger. Dive-bombers hit barges hauling supplies from Corregidor to Bataan. They destroyed food, and our men went hungry more than once.

I watched supply barges leave our anchorage near Cavite, loaded with whatever food we could spare. Sometimes they made it. Sometimes Japanese dive-bombers caught them in open water, and the food we'd loaded ended up on the bottom of Manila Bay with the Filipino crews brave enough to make the run. Every time a barge went down, I calculated what we'd lost...how many men would go hungry because those crates of canned goods or sacks of rice never reached the front lines.

The mathematics of starvation became my constant companion. So many men. So much food. So many meals per day. How long could we last?

Japanese bombers destroyed the U.S. Army bakery near Queens Tunnel, and nobody baked more bread. The bakers, mostly U.S. Army and Filipinos, had done wonderful work trying to produce enough bread for Corregidor and all the Navy and Army ships in the harbor. Often they had loaves in the ovens when Japanese medium bombers came over Corregidor and dropped bombs. Most men dove for air raid shelters and foxholes, but some bakers stuck to their jobs and watched the bread, a choice that proved risky and deadly.

I knew those bakers. We'd traded supplies, shared techniques, complained about our respective commanding officers the way cooks do. They wore Army uniforms and I wore Navy blues, but in the galley we spoke the same language...the language of feeding men who depended on us.

The day the bakery took a direct hit, I stood on deck watching the raid. The Japanese came in at about 20,000 feet...high enough that our anti-aircraft fire couldn't reach them. They flew in perfect formation, twenty-seven bombers in a V, and when they opened their bomb bays it looked like they laid eggs.

The first stick of bombs walked across the bakery. The building lifted straight up, like God grabbed it by the roof, and then it came apart in the air. Pieces of wall, roof, ovens…and men…mixed in a cloud of dust and smoke.

Loaves in the ovens scattered across a hundred yards of Corregidor. One loaf landed in the water near our ship, perfectly intact, still steaming. It floated a moment before a piece of shrapnel from a secondary explosion sliced it in half.

That bread always came out with good texture and taste, well rounded, about two pounds a loaf. When Japanese raids destroyed the bakery, we lost more than a building.

That night I made biscuits in the galley. We'd run out of baking powder weeks earlier, but I made them anyway with what I had. They came out flat and hard, more like hardtack than proper biscuits, but the crew ate every one without complaint.

"These are good, Cookie," one of the gunner's mates said, though we both knew he lied.

"Best I can do," I said.

"Best anybody can do," he replied, and he told the truth.

The U.S. Navy oversaw cold storage and dry stores. We had enough frozen meat on hand to last twenty years, but when Japanese bombers hit the cold-storage plant, the doors jammed, and nobody could get inside the refrigeration rooms.

I joined the crew that tried to open those doors. We worked three days with crowbars and sledgehammers, but the blast twisted the frame so badly the doors welded shut under the force. Inside sat tons of frozen beef, pork, chicken…enough protein to keep every man on Corregidor healthy for months.

By the third day, the smell seeped out. The power lines were cut, the refrigeration failed, and in the tropical heat all that meat turned into a biological weapon. They sealed the building and marked it contaminated.

Twenty years of food, gone in one afternoon.

You could still get shredded coconut and sugar on Corregidor if you went through the Navy Chief in charge of stores. Crews sometimes scrounged enough for chocolate fudge and candy. Baking powder? Nobody had it. Every ship in the harbor and Corregidor ran dry.

I made the trip to see the Navy Chief twice a week, trading cigarettes and favors for whatever I could get. The Chief, a lifer, knew that feeding men kept them fighting. He'd slip me extra sugar when he could, or a can of condensed milk that hadn't been inventoried yet.

"Don't tell nobody where you got this," he'd say, handing over a five-pound bag of rice or a case of canned peaches.

"Never saw you before in my life, Chief," I'd reply, and we'd grin.

With sugar and coconut, I could make something that almost qualified as dessert. The crew called it "Cookie's mystery candy" because they never quite figured out what I put in it. I used whatever I had...coconut, sugar, condensed milk when I could get it, sometimes crushed hardtack for texture, once even medicinal alcohol I boiled hard to burn off the poison.

It wasn't good, but it was sweet, and sweetness tasted like civilization.

Under the tunnel floors, underground storerooms held thousands of canned evaporated milk and mountains of dry stores. In my opinion, we had ten to twenty years of dry stores on hand.

I saw those storerooms once, when I joined a detail hauling supplies. Room after room carved into the rock, stacked floor to ceiling with crates. Canned milk, canned vegetables, canned fruit, flour, rice, beans, sugar, coffee...everything an army needs to hold out indefinitely.

"Why don't they issue more of this?" a sailor asked.

"Because once it's gone, it's gone," the supply officer said. "We're rationing for a siege that might last years."

We all knew the truth. The siege wouldn't last years. Either relief would come, or the enemy would overrun us. Those supplies insured a future that probably wouldn't arrive.

The Japanese Air Force kept bombing the bakery, ice storage, garages, refrigerator rooms, machine shops, parts storerooms…everything. Little by little, they whittled Corregidor down. The situation in the Philippines worsened every day.

Every day something else disappeared. Every day our world shrank. The machine shop where we repaired equipment. The garage where we kept the trucks that moved supplies. The ice storage where we kept what little fresh food remained.

I kept a mental inventory of what we'd lost until the list dragged me under. Better to focus on what still sat on my shelves, what I could still cook, how to feed the crew one more day.

A large freighter named Don Jose anchored near the U.S. Army docks. Earlier in the war she caught fire. After a stubborn battle, crews put it out and a tug towed her to Lands End…the nearest land to the outer ocean…to serve as a decoy for Japanese dive-bombers so Corregidor's gunners could pick them off.

We watched the Japanese bomb that ship every single day for two weeks. They obsessed over it, convinced it still ran. Every morning, like clockwork, a flight of dive-bombers peeled off and dove on Don Jose.

And every morning, our anti-aircraft crews waited.

It became a game, almost. The Japanese came in, our guns opened up, and sometimes we got lucky and knocked one out of the sky. The crew kept score like a baseball game.

"That's three this week," the gunner's mate announced, proud.

Before she burned, Don Jose carried distilled spirits…whiskey, wine, and the rest. Orders said to destroy the cargo, but men smuggled many cases ashore and hid them or drank them.

I may have helped. I may have known about a case of bourbon tucked in the bilge behind the auxiliary pump, wrapped in canvas. And I may have used a shot in the galley from time to time, to fortify the coffee or deepen a soup.

The crew never asked why the coffee carried an extra kick. They drank it and went back to their guns.

Don Jose squatted on a reef, but the enemy didn't know it. Every day the Japanese dive-bombers bombed and strafed, and after several weeks, they couldn't figure out why she wouldn't sink like the others.

"They must think we've got the best damage control in the Navy," one officer joked.

"Or they're just terrible shots," another replied.

Once, a boarding party from the *USS Oahu* (Navy Inshore Patrol) managed to get aboard to inspect damage and possibly salvage something. After a thorough inspection, we found everything burned out. Heat had melted the heavy wire rigging, and the decks collapsed from the fires.

A large lighter of Enfield rifles sat sunken in shallow water very close to Corregidor. Ships sent small boats and launches out, and volunteer crews dove for them. The rifles were packed in cosmoline, which kept them serviceable despite the water. Several thousand were recovered and put back into use—the 1903, thirty-caliber, bolt-action type. Some of those rifles went on to stop a fair number of Japanese.

I joined that party. We rowed over in the middle of the night, climbed the side, and spent two hours searching wreckage by flashlight.

The heat had warped the steel decks. In places, metal had melted and run like water. The galley was gone...just a hole in the deck where it had been.

But in one hold, we found three cases of canned peaches that somehow survived. The cans were blackened, labels burned off, but when we opened one, the peaches inside were perfect.

We brought those three cases back to the *Oahu* like treasure. And they were.

The enemy used tricks to lure American gunboats and minesweepers. At night they turned loose small rafts made from bamboo with a hollow length in the center housing a flashlight and batteries.

The *USS Oahu* and other craft retrieved one of those rafts without using searchlights or firing, and we exposed the trick.

One night I had the midnight to 0400 watch. I made a trip to the fantail to check on the stern watch, came back on the starboard side looking toward Cavite, and almost passed out. About five hundred feet away and fifty feet in the air was a good-sized balloon with a paper lantern suspended beneath it, painted with a grinning skull.

The enemy thought anybody who spotted it would shoot at it. Then they'd fire at the muzzle flash. I didn't shoot. I watched it drift and thought about how much effort someone had put into building a thing like that, and what that said about how the war was going for them.

We hauled that raft aboard and stripped it to see how it worked. Simple: a flashlight, batteries, and a bamboo pole to keep it upright. The Japanese set a dozen adrift and waited for a curious American to hit one with a searchlight.

Then their shore batteries would have a perfect target.

We kept the raft as a souvenir, and I used the bamboo pole in the galley to stir the big soup pot. Every time I used it, I thought about the Japanese soldier who built it, waterproofed the flashlight, calculated the battery life.

He tried to kill us. Now his work helped me feed the crew.

War twisted everything that way.

One late afternoon in March, a strange shape floated toward the *USS Luzon.* Closer in, we saw a body...blown up to two or three times normal size, gray and appalling. A knife-like fin cut the surface and headed for the corpse. The fin struck between the ribs and tore out a chunk...a hungry shark.

I stood on deck when it happened. We all did; we couldn't look away even when we wanted to. The body had bobbed in the water for days, swollen with gas, and when the first shark hit it, the stench rolled across the water and half the crew vomited over the side.

"God...turn away," a seaman gagged beside me, knuckles white on the rail.

Pitts wiped his mouth with the back of his hand. "Sharks don't waste, not out here."

"Who was he?" someone asked, voice thin.

"Doesn't matter now," the coxswain said flatly. "Say your piece and hold your stomach."

Another fin cut the surface. The water boiled.

"We should fish him out," the first man whispered.

The coxswain gave one short shake of his head. "You want three more overboard trying? Keep your feet under you."

Pitts stared a beat longer, then spoke low. "Fair winds, shipmate."

I swallowed hard. "Aye."

Minutes later another shark joined in, and they tore at the body in a tug-of-war. One shark gripped an arm, spun the corpse, and ripped it loose. By then, ten or twelve .30-caliber machine guns laid a withering blast toward the sharks, but they kept tearing as the tide carried the body toward the sea and out of range.

We gave up any thought of swimming right then.

That night nobody wanted fish for dinner. I'd planned canned salmon, but I changed the menu to rice and beans. Nobody complained.

Another kind of man-eater...the large Jewfish with two rows of razor teeth...always prowled around ships in the harbor. They flashed bright colors, like a rainbow, and ran about four feet in length.

Crews from ships around Fort Mills and Corregidor often tried to catch fish to stretch rations and change the diet. A ship's fireman and I decided to try for deep-ocean fish.

We needed protein. The canned meat ran low, and fresh fish would have been a godsend. So Pitts Eberhardt, one of the firemen, and I set out to build a fish trap.

First we asked a machinist's mate in the engine room if we could borrow a large wire-mesh tool-locker door. With solemn oaths to return it soon, we scrambled to the fantail to assemble our trap.

Various crewmen called us crazy and said we wouldn't catch anything. We gathered copper wire and pulled staples and tie-wire from wooden food cases, and we finished the trap in two days.

It looked beautiful, if I say so. A neat wire cube with a funnel that let fish swim in but not out. Filipino fishermen used similar traps, so we figured it would work for us.

Then we discovered we didn't have enough heavy line to lower the trap to the bottom. "We'll just get a few heaving lines," we said, but the boatswain's mate wanted no part of it. He said the lines would fray on the hull and he'd end up short when he needed them.

The boatswain, a crusty old bastard who'd been Navy longer than I'd been alive, took one look and said, "That's the dumbest thing I've ever seen, and I once watched a seaman try to paint an anchor chain while it was deployed."

"It'll work," I insisted.

"It'll sink straight to the bottom and you'll never see it again," he predicted.

He guessed right, but I didn't know it yet.

We hit up a friendly seaman for two heaving lines to use with the trap.

We lowered the trap to the bottom. After an hour we hauled it up to see what we'd caught.

One pilot fish...a dirge in Manila harbor. You can't eat them; they're tough and bony. You need a sharp hatchet to chop them for bait. They carry a mean set of teeth and nip anyone who falls in the water.

"Well," Pitts said, looking at the ugly fish flopping in our trap, "at least we caught something."

"That's not something," I said. "That's an insult."

We hauled the trap up and down a dozen times with no luck and finally chopped the pilot fish for bait.

An hour later, we started the next haul. Halfway up, the line gave. We pulled and pulled until the bitter end came over the rail...minus the trap and one heaving line.

"Oh hell," Pitts said.

"Oh hell is right," I agreed.

How do you explain a missing door to the machinist's mate and a missing heaving line to the seaman?

We went to the engine room first. After small talk, we said, "You know, a funny thing happened to us today."

"Yeah? What was that?" he asked.

"Here's the dope," we said...and told him how we pulled the trap carefully and came up empty, barnacles having frayed the lines so the door now lay in eighty-five feet of water.

He swore and threatened, and we beat a hasty retreat topside.

"He's going to kill us," Pitts said.

"Only if he catches us," I replied.

We knew we'd lose popularity in the engine room and likely lose face with the crew. An hour later, our seaman friend showed up. "I'd like those heaving lines back."

So, we explained the whole disaster again.

He took it better than the machinist. He laughed. "You two are the worst fishermen in the United States Navy."

He wasn't wrong.

"We were just talking about heaving lines," we said. "Bad luck to-day...lost one, the other's badly frayed. But don't worry, we can get two more."

"How?" he asked.

"Soon we'll visit the U.S. Army docks at Fort Hughes. Our friend, the Navy Beach Master, will pull two spares."

That's exactly what we did. The Beach Master at Fort Hughes understood that sometimes you bend rules to keep things running. He handed us two slightly used heaving lines and didn't ask questions.

"Don't tell me what happened to the old ones," he said. "I don't want to know."

"Appreciate it, Chief," I said.

"Just don't lose these," he replied.

We didn't. We gave them back and swore off fishing.

The story traveled fast. For weeks afterward, whenever I served fish for dinner, someone asked, "Did you catch this yourself, Cookie?"

Everybody laughed.

It felt good to laugh. We didn't get many chances.

The *Oahu's* mascot was a gray and white female cat about eighteen months old. She looked a bit down and out, so I decided to catch a pilot fish for her.

Kitty belonged to everyone. She'd been born on the ship and never set paw ashore. She knew every corner of the *Oahu*, every hiding spot, every warm place to sleep.

She'd grown thin. We all had, but watching the cat starve hit hard.

I brought the pilot fish below and called for Kitty. She came running, and the fish gave a twist on the steel deck. Quick as a flash, Kitty pounced...but not for long. The pilot fish smacked her across the head, and she shot away.

I'd never seen a cat move that fast. One moment she pounced; the next she stood ten feet away, offended and confused.

Pilot fish pack a strong skull. Kitty took the hint.

"Sorry, Kitty," I said. "Thought I was helping."

She gave me a look that called me an idiot and stalked off to sulk.

I tried to take the fish topside and heave it overboard, but the stubborn thing suctioned its head to the deck plates. I tied a string to its tail and poured sodium from the ice machine over it. When the fish started thrashing, I lifted it and flung it over the side.

That ended my fishing career.

From then on, I stuck to what I knew: cooking with what I had, making something out of nothing, keeping the crew fed one more day.

That was my war...not the dramatic night raids or heroic gun battles, but the daily grind of feeding hungry men while supplies ran out, equipment broke, and the enemy dismantled the infrastructure around me.

Every morning, I woke up and counted what I had left. Every evening I planned the next day's meals. Every night I lay in my bunk and wondered how much longer we could hold out.

The enemy could bomb us all they wanted. My boys would still eat.

That was my duty. That was my war.

| 8 |

The Last Meal

Bataan fell on April 9, 1942.

We heard it first the way we heard everything by then—a change in the sound. The guns across the water went quiet in a way that wasn't quiet at all. Forty-seven days of artillery and now nothing, and that nothing was louder than anything the Japanese had thrown at us.

Pitts found me in the galley, leaning over a pot that wasn't boiling fast enough.

"Bataan's gone," he said.

I kept stirring. "How bad?"

"Seventy-five thousand men. Maybe more." He sat down on a crate. "Biggest surrender in American history."

I turned the heat up under the pot. It didn't need it.

"Frank."

"I heard you."

"You understand what that means? They'll come for us next. All of them. Every man they had on Bataan comes here."

I understood. Corregidor sat two miles off the Bataan tip—close enough to see the fires still burning on the peninsula. Close enough that the Japanese artillery, now free to move, could set up and reach us with ease. Close enough that what happened to Bataan was going to happen to us. Just a matter of time and angle.

I ladled the soup into the pot anyway. Men still needed to eat.

"How long you figure?" I asked.

"Month. Maybe less."

I said nothing. Went back to the soup.

On the night Bataan finally fell, the *Oahu* led the evacuation. Every Navy craft still afloat formed up astern of us—the Luzon, the Tanager, the Finch, the Mindanao—and we threaded back toward Corregidor through Japanese shore fire that tracked us the whole way. Shells hit close enough to throw spray across the deck. Nobody on the bridge flinched.

I served coffee through it. What else could I do.

When we tied up at Corregidor I stood on deck and watched the Bataan shoreline burning behind us. Those were our men over there now. The ones who'd held out for months on starvation rations and malaria medicine and hope that never arrived.

We'd gotten out. They hadn't.

The guns opened on us the next morning. Not planes this time—artillery from the Bataan ridgelines, the ones we'd been trying to hold for four months. Now the Japanese owned them and they put them to immediate use. The first shell hit somewhere above the Malinta Tunnel and sent a crack through the rock you felt in your back teeth. Then another. Then it was steady and didn't stop.

We ate breakfast to the sound of it.

The fuel ran out in late April.

I didn't know it was coming until the chief engineer appeared at the galley hatch, face gray with something worse than exhaustion.

"How much cooking fuel you got left, Hoeffer?"

I did the inventory in my head. "Week, maybe. If I stretch it."

He nodded like that confirmed something he didn't want confirmed. "Make it last."

The ship's engines had already been dead a week. No fuel to run them. The *Oahu* sat anchored in the lee of Corregidor, a target that couldn't move. They'd left us alone for a few days. Not mercy—they had bigger things to hit first.

When the order came down, an ensign delivered it. Young kid, too young, his uniform already two sizes too big from the weight he'd lost.

"Captain wants all non-essential personnel ashore. You're to report to Battery Geary." He checked his clipboard. "155-millimeter howitzers. You know anything about artillery, Hoeffer?"

"I'm a cook."

"Right." He made a mark. "They'll train you when you get there."

He moved on down the hatch. I stood in the galley a moment, hands on the counter, looking at what I had left. The pots. The one good knife I'd kept sharp all the way from Shanghai. The coffee urn, dented, still running. A half-sack of rice. Some canned goods I'd been saving without quite admitting I was saving them.

Pitts appeared in the hatch. "You hear?"

"I heard."

"Artillery." He said it the way you'd say cancer. "I don't know a damn thing about artillery."

"Neither do I."

We looked at each other.

"When do we go?" he asked.

"Tomorrow morning."

He disappeared. I started cooking.

No particular reason for it. No one had ordered a meal. The ship was half-empty, men already filtering ashore in small groups with their gear. But I had a fire and I had food and I'd been feeding men for five years on this ship and I wasn't ready to stop.

I made rice. Proper rice, cooked slow, not the watery gruel we'd been serving for weeks. I used the last of the salt. Found a tin of corned beef I'd been keeping in the back of the locker behind a false stack of empty cans—I'd hidden it there in December without knowing why, just knowing I should. I opened it and mixed it in.

Kelly came through first, which surprised me. I hadn't seen Kelly in two weeks, thought he'd gone ashore with an earlier detail.

"You're still cooking," he said.

"Somebody has to."

He sat down without being invited. Big jaw, that old scar running white from lip to chin. He'd had it since I first met him in Shanghai and I'd never asked. He looked at the bowl I set in front of him for a long moment before he picked up the spoon.

"Corned beef," he said.

"Last of it."

He ate. Didn't say anything else for a while.

Six men came through in the next hour. I fed them all. Some I knew well, some I barely recognized, faces worn down to something harder and sharper than the faces they'd boarded with in Manila. They ate standing up, sitting on anything available, one man right there on the deck with his back against the bulkhead and his eyes closed while he chewed.

Ah Ting came last. He moved through the hatch quiet as always, that particular stillness he carried everywhere. He'd been through more on this ship than any of us and showed less of it.

He looked at the pot. "Rice?"

"And whatever I had left."

He accepted the bowl. Stood at the counter eating the way he always ate, unhurried, precise. When he finished he set the bowl down and washed it himself in the bucket—he always washed his own bowl—and dried it with a rag.

"You leave tomorrow?" he asked.

"Yes."

He nodded. Reached into his shirt and produced something wrapped in cloth. Set it on the counter.

I unwrapped it. Dried ginger. The same ginger he'd pressed into my hand the day we left Shanghai. For cold seas, he'd said.

"I keep it," he said. "All this time. But I don't need it now." He looked at the port bulkhead, toward Corregidor, the direction of the shore. "You take."

"Ah Ting—"

He shook his head once. That settled it.

I wrapped it back in the cloth and put it in my shirt pocket. He left without another word.

I cleaned the galley that night. The soap smelled like every galley I'd ever worked—that same sharp lye smell that stayed in the cracks of your knuckles for days. I scrubbed the range until the metal was bright, the steel ringing under the brush. Hung the pots in their order. Laid the knives out straight. The sound of it in the empty ship was very loud. Not for whoever came next—no one was coming next. I knew it the same way you know a storm before the barometer tells you. I just needed my hands to keep moving.

I just couldn't leave it dirty.

In the morning I went ashore with a seabag and my knife and the piece of ginger in my pocket.

I didn't look back at the ship. I meant to. But I didn't.

The howitzers were brutal, hot, and loud enough to leave your ears ringing through the night. The crew that trained us had been at it for months and they showed us what to do without ceremony—load, fire, stand clear, load again. Your job was mechanical. The gun did its work and you fed it and that was all.

I was a loader. Not a cook. Not anything I'd been.

The Japanese guns answered ours around the clock. Corregidor took a pounding that made the earlier raids look like practice. The tunnel entrance was choked with men—soldiers, sailors, nurses, Filipino scouts—all of us pressed into the rock while the island shook above us. Outside, the surface of Corregidor was being stripped bare. The trees were long gone. The buildings were rubble. Even the rubble was being ground smaller.

On the morning of May 5th I heard the *Oahu* take her first direct hit.

You know a ship's sound the way you know a voice. Five years on her and the *Oahu* had a particular way of absorbing impact, a metallic complaint in the hull that traveled down through the water. This was different. The shell hit somewhere forward and the sound that came back was wrong—hollow, broken, the sound of something that had given up trying to hold itself together.

I was at the gun and I couldn't leave. We kept firing.

She took more hits through the afternoon. I know because men kept count and the number passed down the line the way all information passed on Corregidor by then, mouth to ear, urgent and quiet. Then: she's going down.

I heard it while I was loading a shell. I pushed it home and stepped clear and the gun fired and the recoil shook my back and I thought about the galley. The pots hanging in order. The knife. The coffee urn, still dented from the storm through the Formosan Straits.

She settled on the bottom in shallow water with part of her hull still showing. The Luzon would go the same day. They'd had plans to scuttle her too, blow the charges and deny the Japanese the prize—but in the end it didn't happen, and the enemy took her whole. The *Oahu* wasn't going to let that happen to her. She'd been a Navy ship her whole life. She went down as one.

Pitts found me that night outside the tunnel entrance. We sat against the rock in the dark. The artillery had slowed but not stopped—it never completely stopped anymore.

"You okay?" he said.

"No."

"Me neither."

We sat a while. Somewhere across the water a fire was still burning on Bataan. It had been burning for weeks. We'd stopped trying to figure out what it was.

"What happens when they take the island?" Pitts asked. He already knew the answer. We all did. He just needed to say it.

"We surrender."

"And then?"

"And then we find out what happens next."

The white flag went up at noon on May 6th.

General Wainwright's order came through the tunnel. All resistance to cease. All American and Filipino forces to lay down arms. The fighting was over.

I heard it and felt nothing particular—not relief, not despair. Just a change in the situation, the way the fuel running out had been a change, the way Bataan falling had been a change. Another door closing. Whatever came through the next one, I had no way to know.

The Japanese came ashore in force. We assembled in our groups and stood in the light and waited for them.

The first guard who walked past me was shorter than I'd expected. Young, face hard, rifle at port arms. He looked at me the way you'd look at cargo—assessing weight and bulk and whether it would be trouble to move.

I looked back at him the same way.

I had nothing left to cook. No galley, no crew, no ship. Five years of knowing exactly who I was and what I did for the men around me, and now none of it.

I put my hand in my shirt pocket. The piece of ginger was still there, wrapped in Ah Ting's cloth.

I left it where it was and waited to find out who I was going to have to be next.

Propaganda and Plunder

In the burnt-out barracks, an old well sat so well hidden the enemy didn't know it existed. The only catch was that the water ran alkaline and brackish.

We found it on the second day. A few of us were poking around the far end of the barracks, looking for anything useful, when one of the men spotted the old stone rim half-buried under debris. We cleared away the rubble and peered down into the darkness. The well dropped maybe thirty feet, and we could hear water at the bottom.

"Think it's good?" someone asked.

"Only one way to find out."

We rigged a rope and a tin can and hauled up some water. It came up cloudy, brownish, and smelled faintly of sulfur. One of the men tasted it and spat immediately.

"Tastes like hell," he said.

"Better than nothing," another said.

Some of the fellows hit upon a novel idea. We had some gas masks on hand, so we disconnected the hose and poured water through the charcoal inside the canister, and nobody noticed any difference in taste.

We tried it. The water came out clearer, but it still tasted terrible...alkaline, bitter, with a metallic aftertaste that lingered on the tongue. Many prisoners drank it anyway, though most of the men decided to hold out until the next day.

I didn't drink it. I'd rather go thirsty than poison myself. But I understood why some of the men did. Thirst does things to a man. It makes him desperate. It makes him take risks he wouldn't normally take.

On the third day, about 10:00 a.m., May 10, 1942, the Japanese called all prisoners out of the burnt-out barracks and told us to assemble.

We stumbled into the sunlight, blinking, confused. Japanese guards shouted and gestured, forming us into two lines. We stood there, waiting, wondering what fresh hell they had in store for us.

The second night, the enemy had 150 cases of dried prunes—U.S. Army property—stacked just inside the entrance to the barracks. The guard must have fallen asleep, because by morning nearly all of it was gone. The men were hungry and figured they would be starved to death anyway.

The enemy was furious. They threatened to shoot whoever had taken them. After much arguing, the Americans denied it. The Japanese ordered a search, found empty cans, and issued an ultimatum: all 150 cases returned by noon or thirty Americans would be shot.

The word went through the barracks. By noon, about fifty un-opened cans came back, plus enough loose prunes to fill two cases. The enemy wasn't satisfied. Thirty or forty men volunteered to face the charges rather than see others taken at random.

The sergeant lined them up and went down the row asking each man how many cans he'd taken. The first man said one can and received several blows on the head with a thick bamboo pole. The next said four cans and got a small tin of corn beef and several cracks on the head. The others said various amounts and all got blows and kicks, some receiving a can of tomatoes or corn beef as absurd reward. The sergeant eventually got tired of hitting and kicking and ordered the men back to quarters.

Then the Japanese doctor decided to throw a scare into the American officers. He forced all officers to stand at attention while he went up and down the row shouting in Japanese. Finally he said in English: "All men make shoot."

Some of the officers nearly fainted.

After a conference with the sergeant, they were told no one would be shot this time. As punishment, no water for the day. Men rigged canvas to catch rain. You didn't stop looking for ways to survive, even when the enemy was actively trying to take everything from you. Especially then.

The big news: the enemy decided to stage a movie-invasion of Fort Hughes for the Japanese News Reel Company.

At first, we didn't understand. Then one guard explained in broken English that we were going to be in a movie...a propaganda film. They wanted to show the world how they had conquered the Americans, how we had surrendered like cowards, how we now belonged to them.

"You...line up. Two line," the guard barked, chopping the air. "Hands up. No smile. No talk."

"What is this?" a prisoner asked, squinting into the sun.

"Movie," the guard said. "News Reel Company. Japan look. All world look."

"A movie?" someone echoed, disbelief edging his voice.

"Yes." The guard nodded hard. "You show surrender. You finish fight. You belong Japan now."

Another guard jogged past with a boxy camera and waved us into place. "Walk slow. Face sad. Look down. No proud."

A man near me snorted. He tried to swallow it, failed.

"Hey!" the first guard snapped, jabbing a finger. "No laugh. Face dead. You lose. Understand?"

"We understand," I said, flat.

An officer stepped up, cap square, jaw tight. "This is victory picture," he announced, searching for words. "Empire show strong. You... how you say... coward surrender." He gave a satisfied nod. "Good. Now we shoot."

The cameraman hunched behind the viewfinder, cranked once, then lifted a hand. "Ready...banzai! Banzai!" The bayonets came up, the line surged, and the guards screamed on cue while we stood there with our hands in the air, trying not to smile.

They ordered us to form two lines about fifteen to twenty feet apart with our hands up, no smiling or talking.

We stood there with our hands raised, trying to look defeated. It wasn't hard. We were defeated...exhausted, filthy, starving, beaten. But the whole setup felt absurd. Japanese soldiers ran around with cameras, shouting directions, staging the perfect shot.

With a great cry of "Banzai!" Japanese soldiers charged through with their bayonets flashing in the sun.

They ran between the lines, screaming, waving bayonets, trying to look fierce and victorious. It was ridiculous. The prisoners looked exhausted, dirty, and ragged, and the act might have worked for the Japanese except we were all laughing, so their show probably looked bad on the screen in Tokyo.

We couldn't help it. It was too absurd. Here we were, starving and beaten, and they wanted us to play along with propaganda. Some men grinned. Others shook their heads. A few laughed outright.

The Japanese guards got angry. They shouted at us to stop laughing, to look serious, to look defeated. The more they shouted, the more we laughed. It was a small act of defiance, but it felt good. It felt like we still had some control, some dignity, even in the midst of all this.

After the act ended, the enemy demanded that we take out all the dry stores on Fort Hughes and load them aboard a small Japanese ship for the journey to Manila.

The laughter stopped. We went back to work. Back to the brutal reality of being prisoners of war.

Most prisoners were weak and could hardly carry anything. We had to climb a very steep hill before we could reach the storerooms, and that climb alone could wear out a man who received only half a canteen cup of water and two spoons per day of catsup or peas.

They assigned me to one of the work parties. We trudged up the hill, legs shaking, breath coming in ragged gasps. The sun beat down. Guards shouted at us to move faster. Some men fell with cases of food on their shoulders the first time.

Guards kicked them, screamed at them, forced them back to their feet. One man, a sailor from the Luzon, collapsed halfway up. He just dropped, the case of canned goods spilling around him. Guards beat him with rifle butts until he got up. He staggered the rest of the way, blood running down his face.

On the second trip for another case, somebody broke open a case of beans, and each man quickly carried some down. On the next trip, cases of tomatoes were broken open and eaten quickly.

We figured it out fast. Guards stood outside the storeroom; they couldn't see what we did inside. So, we started breaking open cases, stuffing food into pockets and shirts, eating as much as we could before we carried the rest down to the docks.

Japanese guards stayed outside and didn't know what we were doing inside. They only cared that stores came out and got loaded aboard the Sanpan at the docks.

We ate beans straight from the can. We ate tomatoes, peaches, anything we could grab. Some men ate so much they got sick. It was worth it. It was the first real food we'd had in days.

This loading of stores lifted most men's spirits.

For a few hours, we had full bellies. We had energy. We felt almost human again. A small victory, but it mattered. It reminded us we were still alive, still fighting, still finding ways to survive.

After we worked until about 4:00 p.m., the enemy told us to quit, and they issued food at 5:00 p.m. About 6:00 p.m., Japanese officers told our American officers that they would transfer all men to Corregidor sometime in the evening and ordered all prisoners to be ready to move.

We gathered our few belongings. Most of us had nothing. A blanket, maybe. A canteen. A few personal items we'd hidden from the guards. We stood in formation, waiting for the order to move.

Around 8:00 o'clock, Japanese guards escorted the men down to the docks and put us aboard lighters for the journey to Corregidor.

The lighters were flat-bottomed barges, crowded and filthy. They packed us in like cattle, shoulder to shoulder, barely able to move. The water lay calm, black, reflecting the stars. In the distance, Corregidor's dark shape rose out of the sea.

In a short time, we reached Corregidor's docks, and guards escorted all of us to our destination, the 92nd Garage.

As we climbed off the lighters and onto the dock, the reality of our situation hit me. This was Corregidor. The Rock. The fortress that was supposed to hold forever. Now the Japanese held it. We were prisoners on our own ground.

As we marched, Japanese guards motioned for men to fall out of line. They quickly searched each man for a wristwatch, money, or any other valuables, then shoved him back into line.

I watched it happen to the man in front of me. A guard pulled him out, patted him down, found his watch, and took it. The man didn't resist. He just stood there, empty-eyed, and let them rob him.

This went on for quite a while, until our men finally passed the word through the ranks to hide all valuables, either by pushing them down into our shoes or, if we wore G.I. khaki pants, by tucking them into the watch pocket the enemy didn't check.

I slipped my watch off and shoved it deep into my shoe. It dug into my ankle, uncomfortable, but I didn't care. I wasn't going to let them take it. It was the only thing I had left from my old life.

The enemy was keen to get American watches, belts, and particularly leather.

They took everything. Belts, shoes, wallets, rings. Anything of value. They picked over us like vultures.

We walked down the steps into the wonderful tunnels with eighty-five feet of solid rock above them, tunnels that stood magnificently under all the Japanese bombs dropped.

I'd been in these tunnels before, during the siege. They had been our refuge, our fortress, our last line of defense. Now they were just another prison.

The road wound around the tunnels and cliffs and gradually worked down to the 92nd Garage. We arrived and guards escorted us into the area and told us to shift as best we could. Most men just looked for a vacant spot and lay down for a little rest until morning.

I found a spot near the back, away from the entrance. The ground felt hard, rocky, uncomfortable. I was so exhausted I didn't care. I lay down, closed my eyes, and tried to sleep.

Around me, men coughed, groaned, and talked in low voices. Some cried. Others prayed. I listened to the sounds of defeat, the sounds of men who had given everything and lost.

We had some type C and D tinned rations on hand, and the guards issued them next morning for breakfast.

We lined up at dawn. The rations were meager...a small can of hash, a few crackers. But it was food. We ate quickly, hungrily, not knowing when we'd eat again.

Japanese guards stenciled numbers on the backs of a good part of the prisoners' shirts and assigned us to groups to draw food.

I got number 347. They painted it on my back with black paint, like I was livestock. Like I was property. It humiliated me, dehumanized me. I didn't protest. None of us did. We stood there and let them mark us.

Every morning, they mustered the groups for work that needed doing around the camp, like digging latrines and cutting firewood for cooking. The Japanese also called for working parties to clean the tunnels...which lay in terrible shape...and allowed us to pick up some clothes if we wanted them.

The tunnels were a mess. Debris everywhere. Broken equipment. Spent shell casings. Blood stains on the walls. We worked in silence, hauling out the wreckage of our defeat.

One morning about 9:00 a.m., the enemy called for twelve radio electricians and radiomen. Here was a job where I might help my country a little more. I didn't know a thing about high-powered transmitters, so maybe I could do some sabotage.

I volunteered immediately. I wasn't a radio electrician. I was a cook. But I figured I could do more damage as a fake electrician than by digging latrines.

Japanese guards put the twelve of us aboard a captured American Army truck and took us to Malinta Tunnel, where the Voice of Freedom radio station was located.

The Voice of Freedom. I listened to it every night during the siege. It had been our lifeline, our connection to the world. Now the Japanese wanted us to dismantle it, destroy it, erase the last symbol of American resistance in the Philippines.

They assigned me to help a U.S. Army radio technician. He asked me to take out a power vacuum tube...a large radio tube...but I didn't know which one, so I told him, "I can't get it out," and he helped me; as I took it out, I dropped it accidentally. At least, that was my story.

The tube shattered on the concrete. Japanese radio supervisors went furious, and I thought they'd kick and beat me, but after a lot of talking and gesturing they accepted it as an accident and sent us back to work.

The Army technician caught on fast. He struggled to free wires, then grabbed wire cutters and snipped them off short.

We worked together and sabotaged as much as we could. We dropped equipment. We cut wires. We broke tubes. We did everything we could to make sure the Voice of Freedom would never broadcast again.

We finally got one transmitter ready to load aboard the captured truck. On the arranged signal we dropped the transmitter, which made the enemy angry again. With threats of "All me shoot," we got it aboard in one piece...but very battered.

Next, we readied a receiver, and we also dropped it off the truck after nearly getting it aboard. This time they gave all of us a good beating, but we had achieved our purposes.

Guards hit us with rifle butts, fists, boots. I took a blow to the ribs that knocked the wind out of me. Another to the face split my lip. I didn't care. It was worth it. Every piece of equipment we destroyed was a small victory.

I figure during that week on the radio station we put most receivers and transmitters out of action...wrecking the large, high-priced tubes and cutting or removing the vital connections.

Sometimes during the day, the enemy detailed two or three men to wander the tunnel. They appointed me to bring out all the small radio receiving sets I could find and take them to the air-conditioned official U.S. Army radio station in Malinta Tunnel.

I found thirty-five radios and managed to jimmy a few. I dropped them or "accidentally" disconnected vital components or shorted circuits...anything to make them useless.

Among the things the enemy recovered were thousands of flashlight batteries, miles of copper wire, rubber and friction tape by the hundred, and 14k pen points.

When I found the pen points, a lot of mail lay around the tunnel, and I picked up a letter. It was addressed to the Post Exchange officer and pleaded for a new 14k Parker or Waterman pen point. The reply said no pen points were available and referred him to a company in Wisconsin.

I read the letter twice. Such a small thing…a pen point. But it represented everything we'd lost. Normalcy, the routine, the simple pleasures of life before the war.

Most desks used by headquarters officers still sat intact, equipment included, even the radio files, which contained copies of every radio message received before surrender.

In an officer's desk I found a restricted map of Luzon showing every gun position and number of guns. I destroyed it immediately.

I tore it into small pieces and stuffed them into my pockets. Later, I flushed them down a latrine. I wasn't going to let the Japanese have that information.

In the officers' desks I found Parker fountain pens, photographic equipment…including expensive cameras…family pictures, letters, keys, .45 caliber guns, pearl-handled automatics, money, rings…everything a man wanted.

I looked at the family pictures. Wives, children, parents. Smiling faces from another world. I wondered if those officers were still alive, if they'd ever see those families again.

I took a couple of hours and read a lot of mail that would never reach its destination. Most letters told of the writer's grim determination to help defend Corregidor to the end.

Service records of Navy men lay scattered all over the tunnel. I saw my own record on the floor, trampled and dirty. I picked it up, looked at it, then let it fall. It didn't matter anymore.

The twelve men working under the Japanese radiomen could pick up anything we wanted in the way of clothing, food, magazines, and any material to build a shelter.

My friend, Pitts Eberhardt, Fireman 1st Class, U.S.N., found a large canvas Army tent, a welcome find since we were living under trees.

We set the tent up, and it gave us a better place to live. We decided to scout for cots and possibly a mattress. We got lucky again, and our new home improved every day.

We scrounged blankets, a small stove, and some cooking gear. We even found a few books and magazines. It wasn't much, but it was ours…a small piece of normal in the chaos.

Whenever rain started, we crammed as many men into our tent as possible.

Rain hammered the canvas and turned the ground to mud. We huddled shoulder to shoulder, trying to stay dry. Some men told stories. Others sang. A few sat in silence, staring at nothing.

While we worked for the enemy dismantling…and sabotaging…the Voice of Freedom radio station, they allowed us several hours off each day. We used those hours well, hunting for things the enemy could use that we could destroy or damage.

We became experts at sabotage. We loosened bolts, contaminated fuel supplies, hid tools. We did anything we could to slow them down, to shave their victory.

After twelve days of work, the enemy told us we would stay at the 92nd Garage until they eventually took us to Japan.

Japan. The word hung in the air like a death sentence. We all knew what it meant. We'd heard the stories…brutality, starvation, disease. Most of us figured we wouldn't survive.

The Japanese radiomen told us they were sorry to be at war with America but now that it had started, they would have to do their duty.

I didn't believe them. They weren't sorry. They were proud. They had conquered us, defeated us, humiliated us. And they were going to make us pay.

They rationed food now according to groups, and we went to our group under Colonel Bunker, U.S. Army.

Colonel Bunker was a good man. He did his best to look out for us, keep rations fair, and keep morale up. There was only so much he could do.

Sanitary facilities ran bad and flies swarmed by the millions. We dug latrines every two days...open trenches thirty feet long and eight to ten feet deep.

The smell was unbearable. Flies were everywhere, crawling on our food, our faces, our wounds. Men started getting sick...dysentery, malaria, infections. The Japanese didn't care. They had no medicine for us, and even if they did, I don't think they would have given it.

Rumors ran through the camp that they would transfer us to Manila. Most men wanted to go; sanitation had gotten so bad that within three or four weeks, many diseases would break out.

We waited. We endured. We survived. And we wondered what fresh hell Manila held for us.

| 9 |

The March to Manila

The day came when the word was passed to break camp. We would go to Manila in an old Japanese freighter.

"About damn time," Eberhardt muttered beside me. "Can't get much worse than this."

We were packed into lighters like sardines and towed to the ship where we climbed aboard to take the 29-mile trip to Manila. The last glimpse of Corregidor would be ours, and we were never to see it again. It certainly was a terrible sight. No trees were standing...just black and brown earth, with everything else flattened.

"Look at it," someone said behind me. "The Rock."

"Ain't much of a rock anymore," another voice answered.

The Japanese freighter stank of fish oil and rust. We were packed into dirty holds, shoulder to shoulder, with barely room to sit. The air was thick and hot. Men coughed and shifted, trying to find space.

"How long you figure?" a sailor asked.

"Twenty-nine miles. Few hours maybe."

"If we don't sink first."

The ship's engines groaned as we pulled away from the island. We thought the freighter would go alongside the docks of Manila, but instead we headed for the beach and dropped anchor. A Japanese landing craft came alongside. All POWs were disembarked.

"Out! Out!" the guards shouted. "Jump!"

About twenty-five feet from the shore we were told to jump out and walk ashore. The depth of the water was about four feet so everybody got good and wet.

"Jesus Christ," Eberhardt said, hitting the water beside me. "It's warm as piss."

Men stumbled in the surf, their shoes filling with sand and seawater. Some lost their footing and went under, coming up sputtering.

"Keep moving!" a guard screamed. "Move, move!"

The place where we landed was five or six miles away from Manila. Our shoes were full of sand and water but the enemy quickly formed us into a line, four abreast, and we were forced marched to Manila.

Most of the guards rode horses although a few walked. The sun beat down. Men began to stagger.

"Water," someone croaked. "Need water."

"Shut up," the man next to him hissed. "They'll beat you."

When we were marching along, the Filipinos tried to give us cigarettes, candy, water…anything they could. But the enemy kicked them and beat them off. Women wept. Old men stood with their hats over their hearts.

"God bless you!" an old woman called out. "God bless America!"

A guard struck her with his rifle butt. She crumpled to the ground.

"Bastards," I heard someone mutter.

There were also some Swedes or Swiss people, but they too were warned away. A blonde woman in a white dress tried to hand a canteen to a sailor near me. A guard struck her across the face. She fell, blood streaming from her nose. The sailor lunged forward.

"No!" Two prisoners grabbed him. "Don't. They'll kill you."

"Let me go!"

"She's alive. You won't be."

In a little while we reached Manila and were forced to march around the city while the enemy humiliated us in front of the Filipinos. If anyone fell down, or failed to move fast enough, he was kicked and beaten.

"On your feet!" A guard kicked a man who'd collapsed. "Up! Up!"

"I can't," the man gasped.

Two other prisoners hauled him upright. "Come on, buddy. We got you."

General Jonathon Wainwright passed us in a big limousine with two Japanese bodyguards. He looked bad.

"That's the General," someone whispered.

"Poor bastard."

"Wonder what they did to him."

The palm trees we passed were full of shrapnel. We also passed the Army Navy YMCA which was being used as a post office and living quarters for Japanese soldiers. Japanese flags hung from the windows.

A Navy chief petty officer had been packing a big burlap bag the whole march. It really appeared to be heavy. He got just inside the gate and fell over dead. He wouldn't need what was in the bag anymore.

Our destination was Bilibid Prison. The men were mustered in a few at a time, and the others had to wait their turn standing up outside. The sun was brutal.

"How much longer?" a man asked.

"Till they say so."

A Filipino constable was standing outside who was supposed to be guarding for the enemy. He got up close to some Americans and said, "Take it easy boy, the Filipinos are all for you and hoping that you will get freed quickly."

"You with them?" someone asked.

"I have to cooperate with the enemy or be tossed into jail and my family harmed," he said quietly. "But we are with you. All of us. Remember that."

"Thanks, friend."

"MacArthur will return," the constable whispered. "We believe this."

After we mustered with the enemy we lined up for food. Giant cast iron pots were full of rice and there was onion soup, which sure did taste good after that march.

"This is it?" Eberhardt said, staring at his bowl.

"Better than nothing."

"Not by much."

The rice was sticky and warm. The soup was thin, but it had flavor. We ate with our hands, scooping the rice into our mouths.

"Tastes like heaven," someone said.

"You got low standards."

We read a sign on a small brick building that read, "Execution Chamber."

Having never sat in an electric chair, I thought I would try it out. It gave me a very uncomfortable feeling while sitting on it. I wondered if the enemy would ever make use of it.

"Well, that's cheerful," Eberhardt said.

"Shut up."

"Just saying."

"You awake?" Eberhardt whispered from the bunk below.

"Yeah."

"Think we'll make it?"

"We made it this far."

"That's not an answer."

"It's the only one I got."

He was quiet for a moment. "That woman. The one they hit."

"I know."

"The Filipinos. They tried to help us."

"They did."

"We're not alone then."

"No," I said. "We're not alone."

I stared at the ceiling and thought about the march, about the Filipinos who'd tried to help us, about the woman who'd been struck down. I thought about Corregidor, burning behind us. I thought about what came next.

We were prisoners now. The war was over for us. But survival...that was just beginning.

| 10 |

The Ten-Man Rule

Aguard came through the barracks one morning and told us four men had tried to escape. They'd headed for Manila. They were caught. He said this the way you'd report the weather—flat, no inflection—and then he told us to assemble in the compound.

We knew what we were assembling for.

They were brought back and chained to posts in front of the Japanese guard barracks. Their hands were tied behind them. A piece of wood was placed between their knees. A length of chain looped around their knees and hands and secured to the post. No hats in the blazing sun. No water. No food.

They were supposed to endure this for seventy-two hours. After thirty-six or forty hours the four men pleaded to be freed or shot. Word had gone through camp that they would be shot regardless.

Before the seventy-two hours were up, a guard came through the barracks again and told us to assemble.

They marched the four men out past us to four shallow graves that had been dug while we were inside. The sun was already hot on the back of my neck. The ground between us and the graves was just dirt, bare and flat, the kind of dirt that holds footprints. Someone had done that work earlier, quietly, without any of us seeing. The graves were already there waiting. That was the part that stayed with me—that those graves existed before the men were brought out, that the whole thing had been planned and prepared like any other task.

I looked at the ground. I let my eyes go soft, unfocused, the way you can make the world blur if you don't want to see it clearly. I had learned to do that in Shanghai, watching things I couldn't stop. You look at a point in the middle distance and you let everything become shapes and light. It doesn't make you blind. It just takes the edges off.

They were given a drink of water and a cigarette. I heard that—the small sounds of men drinking. I didn't watch.

The volley came all at once. Eight rifles. The sound hit the compound walls and came back at us and for a second there was nothing else in the world.

Then one of them started screaming.

I don't know which one. I still don't know. The sound wasn't words—it was just a sound a man makes when his body isn't finished with living and the situation doesn't care. The guards ran forward. More shots, ragged this time, not in formation. The screaming stopped and then started again, lower, and a guard fired once more at close range. Then silence.

The blood had spread wide in the dirt. More than you expect. More than you can prepare yourself for. It darkened the ground around each man and kept spreading even after there was nothing left to drive it. I looked at that and then I looked away and then I couldn't stop looking at it. The flies found it before the guards finished shoveling.

They shoveled dirt on top and marched away.

We were meant to watch. That was the point.

That night I went back to the galley. There was rice to cook for morning. I built the fire and got the pots going and stood over them in the dark while the camp settled around me. My hands did what hands do. The water came to boil. I salted it and added the rice and watched the surface bubble. There was nothing else I could do with that afternoon except put it somewhere and keep moving. Feeding them was the only thing I had left that made sense. So I fed them.

Very soon after, the order came down to organize all American prisoners into ten-man shooting squads.

"All prisoners will be organized into groups of ten men," he declared. "If one man escapes, all ten will be shot. No exceptions. This is the order of the Imperial Japanese Army."

The words hung in the humid air like a death sentence. I looked down the line at the faces around me...gaunt, sunburned, already marked by months of captivity. These weren't men I'd chosen. They were simply the nine souls who happened to be standing near me when the guards counted off. Now one man's decision could get nine others killed.

Something came up the back of my throat—bile, acid, the morning's rice—and burned acrid in my nose. I clenched my jaw and swallowed it back down. Kept my face flat. A guard was watching the line.

That night in the barracks, nobody said much. The man sleeping next to you wasn't just a fellow prisoner anymore. He was your responsibility, your liability, your potential executioner. You stopped trusting, even men you'd known for years.

Before we left the 92nd Garage, a Japanese submarine lieutenant had pulled a group of men aside and told them plainly: they would be taken to Japan and placed in camps surrounded by heavy industries and factories. If the Americans ever bombed Japan, the American prisoners of war would be killed along with the enemy.

Nobody said anything when he told us. There was nothing to say. He wasn't threatening. He was just stating the arrangement.

At Cabanatuan they separated us by trade—truck drivers, bakers, electricians, cooks. The cooks and bakers totaled 126 men. About fifty of us would work the galley.

Our galley master-at-arms was a Marine they called Tiger Jack. He claimed to have once fought Jack Dempsey, and nobody pushed him hard enough to find out if that was true. He ran the galley with the kind of authority that doesn't need explaining.

The problem was the men. While the food was cooking, prisoners would crowd outside and the moment it was done they'd rush in and scoop whatever they could into canteen cups and run. Tiger Jack's job was to stop that. The food was strictly rationed and there wasn't enough of it.

What food there was barely deserved the name. The enemy gave us onions that were alive with maggots. We cooked them anyway—maggots and all—because they were what we had. Once in a while the Japanese killed some pigs and we got the skin, the guts, and the head. They kept the rest. Caribou were killed every week or two and the meat, maybe a thousand pounds, was divided among nine or ten thousand men. Cut into very small pieces and made into soup, it amounted to something you could taste but not feel.

The rice itself was a problem. Green wood made the fires impossible to control. Cooks would start the rice, lose the fire, rebuild it, and the rice would crystallize—raw pockets forming inside the cooked grain, hard as gravel. Men would whistle from outside the galley when that happened, a low mocking sound that meant they knew and the cook knew and everyone was going to eat it anyway.

The worst part of the galley at Cabanatuan wasn't the food. It was the math.

Nine thousand men. Three meals a day. The galley was a long open shed, tin roof trapping the heat until it sat on you like a hand pressing down. Fire boxes along one wall, the smoke going nowhere useful. Every morning I did the same calculation over the same pots—divide this by that, stretch this further, make this nothing into something—and every morning the numbers came out the same way. Not enough. Never going to be enough. The rice smell in the morning was the best thing in the day. The men outside the galley could smell it too. You could hear them shift.

Tiger Jack ran the distribution. That was his job—stand at the serving point and make sure every man got his share and nobody got twice. He was big enough that nobody tested him more than once. A Marine sergeant with hands like shovels and a face that had been broken and reset at least once, probably in a fight he'd started.

"You the cook?" he said to me the first morning.

"I'm the cook."

He looked at the pots. "How much rice?"

I told him.

He did the same math I'd done. His face didn't change. "All right. You cook it right, I'll get it to them right. We'll manage."

It was the word manage that stayed with me. Not enough. Not fine. Manage. He wasn't going to collapse under it. That was clear.

We managed. Some days barely. The rice ran out before the line did on three occasions, and Tiger Jack stood at the serving point and told the men at the end of the line that there was nothing left today. The first time he did it I thought there'd be a fight. There wasn't. The men at the end turned around and walked away, and that was worse somehow—that they'd already learned to accept it, that the outrage had burned off and what was left was just a kind of gray endurance.

"How do you do that?" I asked him afterward.

"Do what?"

"Tell them there's nothing. Keep it from going bad."

He thought about it. "I look them in the eye," he said. "Every man. You look away, they know you're ashamed. You look them in the eye, they know you're not hiding anything. There's nothing left because there's nothing left. That's all."

He picked up his mess kit and went to find whatever rice had stuck to the bottom of the pots.

I'd been in Camp III for five months by then, and during that time nobody had tried to escape from our section. The ten-man squads stayed intact, stayed alive. But Camp I, about four hours' march away, was a different story. Men there were more desperate, or maybe just more foolish. Every few weeks, we'd hear about another attempt.

Sometimes they brought the captured men to Camp III to make an example of them. I remember the first time I saw it. Two Americans, hands tied behind their backs, wearing crude signs around their necks printed in English: "I tried to escape." They stood in the compound while the interpreter lectured us about the futility of resistance.

These two had made it sixty miles to the mountains, he told us. They'd descended to the coast, built a log raft from bamboo and driftwood, and actually reached the Celebes. For a few days, they must have tasted freedom…the open sea, the wind, the possibility of reaching Allied lines. Then they put into a Japanese-held island for water, were captured, and shipped back to the Philippines in chains.

"They will be executed," the interpreter said flatly. "Let this be a lesson to all of you."

They shot them the next morning. We heard the volley from inside the barracks…eight rifles firing as one, then the ragged follow-up shots as each soldier ran forward to empty his weapon into the bodies. It was the Japanese way. They wanted to make sure.

In Camp I, the rumors said, a U.S. Army colonel had been beheaded for attempting escape. I never learned his name, never confirmed if it was true. But we believed it. By then, we'd believe anything.

The Filipinos, though…they never stopped fighting. Japanese Army trucks went out to the countryside regularly to pick up supplies: fruits, vegetables, rice, whatever they could requisition or steal from the local farmers. Filipino guerrillas ambushed these trucks with beautiful regularity. They'd kill the guards, drive the trucks away, and distribute the supplies to the resistance. Sometimes the trucks just vanished, swallowed by the jungle.

At night, the Japanese posted sentries in little wooden huts around the camp perimeter. They'd stand guard for a few hours, then wait for relief. More than once, the relief guard arrived to find his predecessor headless, the body still warm, blood pooling in the dirt. The Filipinos did that work with their heavy bolos…one clean swing in the darkness, barely a sound. The head would roll into the bushes, and by the time anyone raised the alarm, the killer was gone.

The Japanese retaliated, of course. They'd round up natives from the surrounding villages and execute them in batches. It didn't matter if they were guilty. It didn't matter if they were old men or boys. The Japanese needed to kill someone, so they did.

One afternoon in July, a caleso buggy drawn by a weary pony came rattling past the camp fence. The driver was a middle-aged Filipino, weathered and thin, wearing the white cotton shirt and straw hat of a farmer. As he passed, he shouted to us in English: "The enemy will lose the war! The Americans will come back someday and drive the dirty Japanese out!"

We cheered. We couldn't help it. For a moment, the words gave us something we'd almost forgotten…hope.

A Japanese sentry came rushing up, screaming, his rifle raised. He yanked the Filipino off the buggy, beat him with the rifle butt, then dragged him to the guardhouse. We watched through the fence as the officers questioned him, kicking and slapping him between questions. They decided he was dangerous. Dangerous for telling the truth.

They took him to a clump of bushes near the camp, tied his hands behind his back, and shot him. We heard the shots. Later, we saw the shallow grave, the disturbed earth, the pony still tied to a tree with the empty buggy beside it. The buggy stayed there for days, a reminder. Eventually, a Japanese soldier took it away.

The camp had its own economy, its own twisted marketplace. When working parties went outside the fence, Filipino vendors sometimes appeared with goods to sell…cigarettes, sugar, fruit, whatever they could scrounge. The Americans were so desperate for anything different, anything that wasn't rice and thin soup, that they'd offer ten or twenty times the normal price.

At first, the Filipinos sold fairly. But when a man shoves a twenty-peso note in your hand and says, "Give me that pack of cigarettes," you learn fast. It didn't take long for the vendors to realize they could charge whatever they wanted. A few times, a Japanese soldier intervened and forced them to cut their prices, but mostly the guards didn't care. They found it amusing.

The cheapest thing you could buy was a block of brown sugar, formed like a saucer, sold for three centavos…about a cent and a half in American money. This wasn't real sugar. It was the refuse from Filipino sugar mills, the sludge that collected at the bottom of the refining tanks…dirt, straw, molasses, all pressed together and dried. Normally, they sold it as feed for caleso ponies.

In the markets, these blocks sat in open stalls, covered with flies. Thousands of them, buzzing and crawling.

"Three centavos," the vendor said, swatting half-heartedly at the cloud.

"For that?" Pitts muttered beside me. "Looks like somebody scraped a floor and baked it."

"It'll burn in tea," I said. "If we had tea."

He pinched a corner between finger and thumb. "Feels like hoof glue."

The vendor pushed the block closer. "Strong. Sweet. Good." He smiled, teeth stained the color of the sugar.

"Sweet," Pitts said, dry. "Sure."

A boy darted in with a palm fan and drove the flies off in a black wave that settled right back down. "You buy?" he asked.

"We buy," I said, counting out coins, each one a little piece of pride shaved off. "Two."

"Three," Pitts said. "If we're going to sin, let's sin proper."

The vendor wrapped them in old newsprint. The ink bled where the molasses sweated through. "For pony," he added, nodding.

"For sailors," I said.

Pitts snorted. "Close enough."

We stepped away from the stall. Flies followed like we owed them money.

"Don't bite it," I told him. "Shave it."

He scraped at the edge with a mess-knife. The shavings fell like brown bark. He put one on his tongue, chewed, and made a face. "Tastes like the stable smells."

"Dirt, straw, molasses," I said. "All we're missing is the pony."

"You're the cook," he said. "Make it respectable."

"I can melt it." I held a sliver in my palm. Sticky film, grit under the sweetness. "Maybe boil it, skim the top."

"Skim what? The flies or the farm?"

"Yes," I said.

He laughed once, a sound with no joy in it. "We used to put sugar on oatmeal."

"We used to have oatmeal."

He tucked a block into his blouse like contraband. "Think the guards will take it?"

"They take belts," I said. "They'll take this."

"We'll eat it before they look."

"That's the plan."

We walked past more stalls...fish blinking in the heat, greens wilted to rags, a basket of eggs that smelled like the end of the world. The sugar blocks lay in stacks like little gravestones, each one humming with flies.

"That what we are now?" Pitts asked, nodding at the pile.

"Cheapest thing you can buy," I said.

"That what we eat," he said.

"That's what we eat," I answered.

Some men boiled the sugar and strained it through cloth to get the worst of the filth out. Others just ate it as it was, dirt and all. When you're hungry enough, you stop caring.

Besides food and medicine, the thing men wanted most was cigarettes. They craved them, died for them, sold their souls for them. Men would trade their food rations for a few smokes, hastening their own deaths. I watched it happen again and again...men growing thinner, weaker, their eyes hollow, but always with a cigarette between their lips.

Some enterprising prisoners made little squares of candy from hoarded sugar and sold them for cigarettes or cash. It was a brisk trade. For a while, we had small buns issued with our rations, and men would trade one bun for four cigarettes. They'd give up food...actual nutrition...for tobacco. The cigarette was king.

The civilians in camp fared better than the rest of us. They had money, connections, ways to get food smuggled in from outside. They'd sell it at outrageous prices...ten pesos for a pie, twenty pesos for a roast chicken. If you had cash, you could survive. If you didn't, you starved.

Medical supplies were almost nonexistent. We had only what men had managed to carry from Corregidor...a few bandages, some iodine, aspirin if you were lucky. The Japanese had captured tons of medical supplies when the fortress fell, but they kept it all for themselves.

Pellagra spread through the camp like wildfire. It was a vitamin deficiency disease, caused by lack of B2. You could recognize it by the rash, the red inflamed skin, the way the skin peeled off in sheets. Some men had it so bad they couldn't swallow water or eat. Their throats were raw; their mouths covered in sores. They just wasted away.

The Japanese made no effort to help. They had the medicine. They just wouldn't give it to us.

I watched men die from pellagra, from dysentery, from infections that could have been cured with a single shot of penicillin. They died slowly, in pain, surrounded by other men who could do nothing but watch.

And through it all, the ten-man rule hung over us like a sword. Every morning at roll call we stood in our groups of ten in the open compound, the sun already working on us before 0700, and counted off in Japanese. Ichi, ni, san—your mouth making the sounds while your eyes moved down the line, counting bodies, making sure. Every night the same. Not out of friendship. Out of survival. If one man ran, we all died.

In the end, nobody in my ten-man squad tried to escape. We were too afraid. Not of dying...we were dying anyway. We were afraid of taking nine other men with us.

Americans in Camp I were dying at about a hundred a day. Mass burials were in effect—trenches six feet deep and twenty feet long, bodies thrown in mostly without their clothes. The men had dysentery, malaria, tropical ulcers, malnutrition—things that could have been treated with medicine the Japanese had and wouldn't give them.

We heard the numbers and did not talk about them much. Talking about it didn't help anyone.

Escape was almost impossible anyway. The half-Japanese, half-Filipino men the prisoners called jenaps were well armed and would shoot any prisoner on sight. A reward of fifty pesos was paid for any prisoner caught. Fifty pesos. That was the going rate.

Fear is the most efficient guard of all.

| 11 |

The Hell Ship

We all went inside the Port Terminal and found a place to sleep on the cold concrete decks. The building reeked of diesel fuel and rotting fish, and grime slicked the floor. Men shuffled through the cavernous space, searching for any spot not already claimed by another body. I dropped my small bundle of belongings and sat down hard, my back against a concrete pillar that still bore shrapnel scars.

Around me, men settled in wherever they could find space. Some talked in low voices. Others stared at nothing, eyes hollow. A few curled up on bare concrete and closed their eyes.

After we located our spots, the word passed around to fall in for chow. The meal consisted of dry fish ground into tiny particles and steamed rice. They had pulverized the fish so fine it looked like gray dust, and it tasted like salted cardboard. But it was food, and we were hungry.

The line crawled. Too slowly. Men shoved forward, shoulders driving into the man ahead. Some slipped through the line twice, faces blank, not even looking ashamed about it. The Japanese guards didn't notice or didn't care. By the time I got my portion, the rice had nearly run out. Most of us missed rice entirely and got only ground fish for supper. I scooped the fish powder into my mouth with my fingers and tried not to think about what it might have been before they ground it up.

That night, I lay on the concrete and listened to the sounds of fifteen hundred men trying to sleep in a warehouse. Coughing. Groaning. The shuffle of feet heading to the latrine buckets in the corner. Somewhere in the darkness, a man wept quietly. Another man told him to shut up.

I didn't sleep much.

Next morning, October 8, about 10:00 a.m., guards ordered us to fall in. The word came down: we were boarding the ship. We proceeded to embark aboard an old Japanese freighter converted into a transport. The ship's name was the *Totoru Maru*, and she looked like she'd been sailing since the last century. Rust streaked her hull. Her superstructure stood battered and stained. She sat low in the water, listing slightly to port.

She was an old pre-war tub with about a million rats squeaking and running around below decks, rattling paper, gnawing on the wood slats. At night you could hear them over everything else.

For the first part of the voyage they issued us small bags of oyster crackers, one bag per man per meal. Three bags a day. What we didn't know until someone figured it out was that the enemy had packed the crackers in tin boxes that had previously held bars of soap. The crackers were thoroughly impregnated with the taste of soap. Men traded them off for cigarettes as soon as the word got around.

The tonnage of this ship was 7,000 tons, and they were packing 3,000 American prisoners and nearly 4,000 Japanese troops aboard. I did the math in my head. Seven thousand men on a ship built for maybe a tenth of that. It was going to be hell.

They packed the American prisoners into the forward holds like sardines while Japanese troops occupied the after-holds. We shuffled up the gangway in a long, slow line, guards shouting at us to move faster. At the top, a Japanese sergeant stood with a clipboard, counting us off. His face stayed blank, indifferent. We were cargo to him. Nothing more.

I descended the ladder into the forward hold, and the stench hit me like a fist. Sweat. Urine. Vomit. The smell of too many men crammed into too small a space. The hold lay dim, lit only by a few weak bulbs strung along the overhead. Men had already filled all bunk spaces, and bodies covered every bit of deck. Men sat shoulder to shoulder, knee to knee, with barely room to breathe.

I found a spot near the bulkhead and sat down. The steel pressed cold against my back. Around me, men settled in with grim faces. We all knew what this was: a hell ship. We'd heard the stories from guys transferred before. Crews packed ships so tight men suffocated. Our own planes bombed unmarked transports. Ships went down with all hands.

"How long you think this trip's gonna be?" the guy next to me asked. His name was Miller, a Marine from Ohio. A scar ran across his cheek from shrapnel at Corregidor.

"Week, maybe," I said. "If we're lucky."

"And if we're not?"

I didn't answer.

The ship didn't leave right away. We sat in the hold for hours, sweating in the heat. The temperature climbed as the day wore on. Men stripped down to their skivvies, but it didn't help. The air turned thick and wet, hard to breathe. Some guys started to panic, gasping for air that wasn't there.

"Calm down," I told one kid who was hyperventilating. "Breathe slow. In and out. You're okay."

He wasn't okay. None of us were. But he nodded and tried to slow his breathing.

Finally, late in the afternoon, the ship's engines rumbled to life. The deck vibrated beneath us. We felt the ship begin to move, pulling away from the pier. Through the small hatch above, I saw a sliver of sky. It was the last daylight I'd see for a while.

We viewed Corregidor from the water as we passed—an awful sight, all battered and burnt. We also saw Fort Drum, which still looked impressive with its 14-inch guns in turrets. Talk was that those guns had killed whole Japanese divisions. They didn't look beaten. They just looked abandoned.

The first night was the worst. The hold turned pitch black except for the dim bulbs, and the heat smothered us. Men groaned and shifted, trying to find a position that didn't hurt. The latrines were just buckets in the corner, and within hours they overflowed. The smell became unbearable.

I tried to sleep, but it was impossible. Every time I closed my eyes, I felt the press of bodies around me, the weight of the ship above me. I kept thinking about the water outside, the ocean that could swallow us whole if the ship went down. We were trapped. If anything happened, we'd drown like rats in a barrel.

Around midnight, a fight broke out. Two guys argued over space, their voices rising until fists started flying.

"You're on my blanket."

"I got nowhere else."

"Move your damn feet."

"Make me."

A shove. A thud. Someone hissed, "Knock it off," and someone else, "Save it."

Boots hit the ladder. The guards came down.

"Yameru! Quiet!"

"Back! Back!"

Rifle butts cracked bone.

"Onna...stop, he's..."

"Shut it!"

They beat them both until they stopped moving. After that, the hold went quiet except for the sound of men breathing and the creak of the ship's hull.

In the dark beside me, Miller whispered, "Not worth it."

"Nothing down here is," I said.

The days blurred together. We got two meals a day, if you could call them that...rice and soup, passed down through the hatch in buckets. Worms infested the rice, and the soup was just hot water with a few vegetables floating in it. We ate it anyway. Hunger made everything taste good.

The worst part was the thirst. We got one canteen of water per day, and it never sufficed. Men hoarded their water, sipping it slowly to make it last. Some guys drank it all at once and spent the rest of the day begging for more. The guards laughed at them.

On the third day, a man died. He’d boarded sick—dysentery or malaria—and the hold finished him off. By the time he went, the smell in that enclosed space was already beyond description, and then it got worse. His body lay in the corner for hours, the men nearest him shifting away as far as the crowd allowed. Nobody said anything. The guards finally hauled it up on deck. We didn’t know what they did with it. They probably just tossed it overboard.

After that, more men started to die. One or two a day. The guards stopped caring. They came down, dragged the bodies out, and that was it. No ceremony. No prayers. Just gone.

I kept my head down and tried to stay alive. I rationed my water. I ate every scrap of food they gave me, no matter how rotten. I kept moving, stretching my legs when I could, keeping my blood flowing. Some guys just gave up. They stopped eating, stopped drinking. They lay down and waited to die. I couldn’t let myself do that.

Miller, the Marine, stayed close to me. We watched out for each other. When one of us got weak, the other propped him up. When guards came through looking for trouble, we kept our heads down and stayed quiet. We survived by staying invisible.

On the fifth day, the ship stopped. We heard activity on deck, shouting, and the thud of cargo shifting. Word came down that we were at a port, but we weren’t getting off. They were just taking on supplies. We sat in the hold and waited.

That night, the ship started moving again. The engines rumbled, and we felt the sway of the open ocean. Some guys got seasick, vomiting into the already overflowing latrine buckets. The smell defied description.

I lost track of time. Days and nights blended together in the darkness of the hold. I slept when I could, ate when they fed us, and tried not to think about how much longer this would last.

On the fourth day out of Manila, a great cry went up from the Americans on topside. Torpedoes. Two distinct wakes coming from the port side.

The men who could see them started shouting. The Japanese captain was on the bridge and the Americans managed to get his attention. He swerved the ship out of the way.

We were not molested again. Both Americans and Japanese were glad of it. There was approximately one life jacket to every five men aboard.

Finally, after what felt like an eternity, the ship slowed. The engines changed pitch. We heard activity on deck again…more shouting, the clang of metal on metal. The hatch opened, and light poured in, blinding after so many days in the dark.

Before we docked at Formosa, they lined us up for a dysentery examination. The Japanese medical attendants had a long glass rod, about ten inches, thin as a thermometer with a small hook at the bottom. They pushed it into the rectum of each man, twisted it, and withdrew it. The end was then rubbed onto numbered glass slides placed in wooden boxes.

They did this at every port. It was not pleasant.

"All prisoners, prepare to disembark!" a guard shouted down.

We climbed the ladder slowly, our legs weak from days of sitting. When I reached the deck, I squinted against the sunlight. The air hit cold, shockingly cold after the heat of the hold. I took a deep breath and tasted salt and freedom.

We stood in Korea. Fushin, they told us. The port bustled with ships and cranes, and in the distance, hundreds of smokestacks belched black smoke into the gray sky. Steel smelters, I figured. And shipyards. Dozens of ships under construction.

They ordered over 1,300 Americans to disembark at Fushin for work in Mukden, Manchuria. After the men landed and mustered, the guards issued coats with fur on the bottom. It was November, and the cold bit through our thin clothes like knives. The remaining Americans would travel on to various ports and cities in Japan.

I watched men file off the ship, their faces gaunt and hollow. Some could barely walk. Others rode stretchers. I wondered how many of us would survive whatever came next.

Miller stood beside me, shivering in the cold. "We made it," he said.

"Yeah," I said. "We made it."

But I knew the worst still lay ahead.

| 12 |

Osaka

few days before docking, the sick men...maybe a hundred of them...had been told they'd be taken to hospitals. I doubted the quality of care they'd receive, but at least they'd be off the ship. During the voyage from Formosa to Korea, we'd buried nine more men at sea. The Navy Chaplain had performed the services, the American flag draped over each body before it slid into the water. Sixteen dead total since leaving Manila. Sixteen men who'd survived Corregidor only to die in the hold of a Japanese transport.

The *Totoru Maru* left Fushin and headed for Mojie. As we passed through the port, no Americans were allowed above decks. Only a few men could go to the latrines, and through cracks in the wooden structures, I caught glimpses of old temples and fishing boats. Nothing more. The Japanese weren't taking chances.

After Mojie, we entered the Inland Sea. The water changed color—greener, calmer, sheltered by the islands that rose on either side. The air had a different smell to it, pine and something else, cold and mineral, nothing like the Philippines. Japan. I stood on deck with the wind off the water cutting through my shirt and watched the coastline go past. Fishing villages. Terraced hillsides. Smoke from somewhere inland. A country that had never heard of me, that I was now going to spend years inside.

On November 11, 1942, at ten o'clock in the morning, we docked. My legs were wrong after thirty-five days at sea—the ground didn't move and my body kept expecting it to. The cold hit us the moment we came off the ship, a dry Japanese November cold with a wind coming off the hills that found every gap in your clothes. Thirty-five days. Sixteen dead on the crossing. I walked down the gangway and put my feet on Japanese soil and tried to remember who I was before all of this.

I saw Sergeant Coleman before they took him off. The man was swollen up like a balloon from beriberi, his skin stretched tight and shiny. But he could still walk, and he was cheerful, cracking jokes with the men around him. Nearly everyone agreed he was in very bad condition. I wondered if he'd make it a week.

November 11 was chilly in Osaka Harbor. I stood on deck in my Filipino summer clothes, shivering. Most of the men were suffering from pellagra, malaria, or just plain cold. Our skin was flaky and discolored, our bodies weak from months of inadequate food. Before noon, the word was passed for all Americans on the list for Tokyo to fall in. Trucks waited to take them to the railroad station.

The rest of us...me included...were mustered and marched off the ship. Japanese Home Guards met us at the dock, squawking orders in broken English. "Four's! Four's! Fall in to the columns of four's!"

Then came the surprise. A light-skinned, well-built Japanese man stepped forward with a typed master list and began reading off names in nearly perfect English. After thirty-five days of Japanese barked at us like we were livestock, hearing those vowels come out clean and flat and American stopped me cold. His accent was minimal. I learned later that the man had spent a good number of his school years in America.

"I am Fujimoto," the interpreter said. "I am the interpreter for Osaka No. 1 prisoner of war camp. You will march approximately two miles. Food will be waiting for you there."

We would later call him "The Thug." But on that first day, he seemed almost professional.

We marched through Osaka in the cold. My feet were numb in my thin shoes, my body shaking. Forty-five minutes later, we arrived at what would be our home for a long time. The camp sat in an industrial area, surrounded by warehouses and factories. Exactly where the submarine lieutenant had said we'd be placed...surrounded by heavy industry so that if the Americans ever bombed Japan, we prisoners would die along with the enemy.

Fujimoto got down to business right away. "Unpack your belongings. Lay out all knives, razor blades, and scissors for inspection."

This happened in the street opposite the camp. One of the Japanese guards held a large wooden box, and we filed past, dropping our contraband inside. Fujimoto told us the items would be returned later. Surprisingly, they were.

After inspection, Fujimoto gave orders to march to the camp staff recreation grounds. We shuffled forward, exhausted and cold. When we arrived, the Japanese guards shouted, "Kyoski!"

Attention.

Out of one of the wooden barracks came an old man dressed in a Japanese colonel's uniform. I stood at attention, wondering what was coming. The colonel started shooting off his mouth with a lot of "Nippon Wa." The country of Japan. I caught enough words to understand the gist before Fujimoto translated.

"You are now in Japan. Here you will stay until the war is over. Papers have been prepared for you to sign. They must be signed or you will be shot by our guards."

The papers read: I will not attempt to escape. If I do, I shall be severely punished.

After signing, we had to line up and run past the Japanese colonel, saluting him in proper Japanese fashion. My belongings banged and rattled as I ran. The colonel watched each man with cold eyes, and if the salute wasn't snappy enough, he made the prisoner do it over and over again. That colonel was a fanatic when it came to saluting. We found that out fast.

Finally, we were allowed to march to our quarters. There were about two hundred Americans from Wake and Guam already in the camp. The total number of prisoners was 632...Chinese, Norwegians,

Italians, Spaniards, Englishmen, Scots, Welsh, Australians, and one Franco refugee.

We were served steamed rice and onion soup. It was hot, and it tasted very good. Some of the Americans were so sick they gave most of their food away. Others ate so much they got what we called "bloated guts"...a tight, painful feeling around the stomach. I ate slowly, savoring each bite. I'd learned on the ship that eating too fast after starvation could make you sicker than not eating at all.

Our rations, Fujimoto explained, would be 700 grams of rice, 250 to 450 grams of vegetables, and 5 grams of sugar per month. Officers would receive ten packs of cigarettes, enlisted men seven packs. These rations would gradually be reduced to eleven cigarettes and half a pack of hair tobacco every fifteen days.

I was assigned to a room thirty-three feet long, approximately twenty-seven feet in height and width. The bunk spaces consisted of three floors, each about six feet six inches apart. Each man received a new mat woven from straw, about the thickness of linoleum, five gray blankets woven from similar material, two bowls, and one fork and spoon.

Every room had a man detailed as room leader. He was supposed to act as a go-between for the enemy and the men he was in charge of. I was glad I wasn't chosen. The room leaders caught hell from both sides.

At eight o'clock every night, we had tenko...roll call. All men had to sit up in their bunk spaces with their legs crossed under them, hands placed on our knees, head held erect, eyes looking straight ahead. The first man on the bottom shelf would start counting off in Japanese. If anyone got mixed up, the Japanese duty officer would strike the man with the handle of his sword. Then he'd order the man down and command him to count in Japanese up to one hundred, sometimes for several hours, while standing at attention.

If a man wasn't present for roll call, regardless of his reason, he'd be subjected to severe punishment...standing on his knees or being slapped around by the guards. Sometimes the guards slapped prisoners just for their own amusement. The Japanese military men humiliated us at every chance they got. To them, prisoners were the lowest persons in the world and should be subjected to all kinds of indignities.

About two days after arriving at Osaka, Fujimoto came into our room and asked who would like to volunteer for work. Only a few men expressed willingness. Fujimoto said nothing but added that American Red Cross parcels would be issued soon. Also, we'd receive a small white face towel, tooth powder, and a toothbrush.

We would learn later what "soon" meant in Japan. It could be a day, days, months, even years. Nothing definite.

Quite a few of the Americans suffered from beriberi, pellagra, ulcerated sores, and eye diseases. The enemy was quick to notify all room leaders that sick men would receive only half rations while workers received full rations.

By November 14, a little better than half of the newly arrived prisoners were working. The work consisted of carrying heavy weights, some by a stout pole called a yo-ho pole, about five feet in length and two and a half inches wide in the center, tapering down to one inch at the ends. Two men would sling the pole over their shoulders with baskets suspended in the center. These baskets would hold about seventy kilos...154 pounds.

I volunteered for work. Not because I wanted to, but because half rations meant slow death. I'd seen it on Corregidor, seen it on the ship. Men who stopped eating stopped living. It was that simple.

The first morning I went out to work, I stood in the cold at six-forty, waiting for the camp leader to shout, "All hands! Fall out the working parties!" We were supposed to run to the gate on the double and salute the guards on the way out. The Japanese camp commander was often present, and he expected a good salute. Anyone caught failing to salute would be the luckless victim for that day.

I learned to salute properly. I learned to count in Japanese. I learned to bow at the right angle, to keep my eyes down, to move quickly when ordered. I learned that survival in Osaka No. 1 meant becoming invisible, unremarkable, just another prisoner in summer clothes shivering through a Japanese winter.

And I learned that the war was far from over.

| 13 |

First Christmas in Hell

December 1942 had come. The barracks at night were cold in a way that got into your joints and stayed there—a damp Japanese winter cold, different from anything back home. You could hear men shifting in their bunks, the creak of wood, someone coughing at the far end of the room, somebody else muttering in his sleep. I lay staring at the wooden slats above me and thought about Christmas. My mother's kitchen. The smell of it. Turkey and sage and something sweet in the oven. Whether they knew I was alive.

The prisoner of war in charge of the camp galley was a quartermaster in the Royal Artillery, HRM Army. His name was Davies, and he'd been requesting the enemy to give him a quantity of food so all the men could have a special Christmas dinner. I watched him approach Fujimoto day after day, bowing at the proper angle, speaking in careful, measured tones.

"Please, honorable interpreter-san," Davies would say. "Christmas is very important holiday for Western men. Small extra ration would help morale very much."

Fujimoto would wave him away. "No extra food. You eat what is given."

But Davies was persistent. He understood something about the Japanese that many of us didn't...they respected persistence, as long as it was wrapped in proper deference. The enemy was very reluctant to give any extra food, but they did finally submit after repeatedly being asked for it.

About the 15th of December, Davies came into our room with a conspiratorial look on his face. "We've got one bag of potatoes," he whispered. "Taken from the issue and put away for Christmas. I've requested more greens to cover the withdrawal."

"You're a bloody genius," one of the Englishmen said.

"Or a bloody fool if they catch you," another added.

By the end of the 23rd of December, enough extra rice, sugar, and potatoes were on hand to ensure a fairly large meal on Christmas day. The Japanese supply officers had made a vague promise that an International Red Cross food parcel might be issued for Christmas, and everybody was anxiously awaiting results from this promise.

I didn't believe it. I'd learned by now that Japanese promises meant nothing. "The near future" could be tomorrow or never. But I kept my mouth shut. Hope was a fragile thing in Osaka No. 1, and I wasn't going to be the one to crush it.

All was a bustle in the galley two days and nights before Christmas. I volunteered to help, partly to stay warm, partly to be near the food. The galley was the warmest place in camp, with the cooking fires going constantly. Davies had me peeling potatoes...real potatoes, not the half-rotten vegetables we usually got.

"How many men we feeding?" I asked.

"Six hundred thirty-two," Davies said. "Give or take a few in the stadium."

The stadium. That's what we called the hospital...a former baseball stadium where sick men went to die. I'd heard stories about the place. No medicine. Half rations. Japanese doctors who seemed to enjoy watching men suffer.

"We sending anything special up there?" I asked.

Davies nodded. "Double portions if I can manage it. Those poor bastards need it more than we do."

Friday, December 25, 1942, was Christmas day. At 06:30 a.m., reveille was sounded. This was to be our first Christmas in Japan, and a very strange one too. I stood at attention in the cold, my breath forming clouds in the morning air. The Japanese duty officer walked past, inspecting us with cold eyes.

"Kyoski!" he barked.

We snapped to attention.

After roll call, word spread through the camp like wildfire. "Red Cross parcels! They're issuing Red Cross parcels!"

I couldn't believe it. The Japanese supply officer was actually issuing one Canadian Red Cross box to every three men and one International Red Cross parcel to every two men. The enemy always fixed it up for the prisoners to split nearly everything issued to take out most of the enjoyment of the issue. They were very cunning and cruel that way.

But we didn't care. We crowded around the supply room, the press of bodies warmer than anything we'd felt in weeks. When I finally got my share I stood there holding the boxes and my hands were shaking. Not from cold. The cardboard was smooth and solid and real. I opened the Canadian box slowly—canned meat, chocolate, cigarettes, powdered milk. I held the chocolate bar and smelled it before I put it away. Butter. A small tin of actual butter. I didn't open it right away. I just held it.

"Look at this," my bunkmate said, holding up a can of Spam. "Real meat."

"Split three ways," I reminded him.

"Still better than fish-head soup."

Christmas day was cold, but braziers were going full blast in every room. Men were cooking up concoctions from rice and Red Cross food, trading items, sharing recipes. The smell of real food filled the barracks...chocolate melting, meat frying, coffee brewing. It was almost enough to make you forget where you were.

An issue of jam was also received by the prisoners. Two pounds for every sixty-six men, which amounted to approximately two teaspoons per man. I savored mine slowly, letting the sweetness sit on my tongue. I couldn't remember the last time I'd tasted something sweet.

Among the other articles we received that day was one pack of Camel cigarettes and one bar of Japanese face soap called Cow Brand. A picture of a milk cow was stamped on the bar. It was fairly good soap, better than the fish-oil stuff we usually got.

The Japanese duty officer came into our room around noon. We all stood and bowed.

"You not work today," he said in broken English. "But Sunday, you work. Make up for today."

We'd expected as much. The enemy never gave anything without taking something back.

All enjoyed Christmas, but of course all men were thinking of their loved ones at home and inwardly yearning to be with them. I sat on my bunk in the afternoon, eating my small portion of Christmas dinner...rice mixed with canned meat, a spoonful of jam, a piece of chocolate. It was the best meal I'd had in months, but it tasted like ashes in my mouth.

I thought about my mother's Christmas dinners. Turkey with all the trimmings. Mashed potatoes with gravy. Pumpkin pie. My sister's laugh. My father's terrible jokes. The smell of pine from the Christmas tree.

"You all right, Frank?" someone asked.

I wiped my eyes. "Yeah. Just the smoke from the brazier."

The first Christmas wasn't so bad as the Japanese had everything they wanted. No doubt the next one would be to the contrary. Would that date bring us nearer to being liberated, or would we be just as far off as we were now? We pondered the situation.

That night, a group of us sat around the brazier, talking in low voices.

"War'll be over by next Christmas," one man said confidently. "Mark my words."

"You're dreaming," another replied. "This'll go on for years."

"I say 1944," someone offered. "Maybe early '45."

One man…a quiet sailor from California…said, "July 1945."

We all laughed at him. "You're crazy. That's three years away."

"Just a feeling," he said, shrugging.

He was ridiculed as a crepe-hanger and crazy, but he'd turn out to be almost right.

Some men were sure, in their minds, when the war was going to end. However, when the time came and passed, they were very disappointed and thought it would never end. Morale was very high in the camp, despite everything. The enemy tried every trick they knew to break the prisoners down, but we held together.

A few days after Christmas, the Japanese issued questionnaires to all the prisoners. It was compulsory to answer them. I sat on my bunk, reading through the questions with growing irritation.

Former occupation?

Cook.

Education level?

High school.

What is your opinion on who will win the present war and how?

I thought about lying, about telling them what they wanted to hear. But something in me rebelled. I wrote: America will win through mass production and air supremacy.

Most of the prisoners gave similar answers. We weren't going to give the enemy the satisfaction of pretending we believed their propaganda.

The Japanese duty officer collected the questionnaires and read through them. His face darkened with anger.

"You are wrong!" he shouted through the interpreter. "Japan will win war! Japanese fleet will sail into New York harbor for review!"

We all figured that the Japanese fleet would have as much chance of entering New York as a snowball in hell, but we kept our faces blank and said nothing.

Every day the enemy issued propaganda and was unconsciously building themselves up to be the world's greatest and biggest liars. Every chance the enemy got, they ridiculed the late President of the

United States, Franklin Delano Roosevelt. In the Nippon Times, which was the official Japanese Army organ, they had a picture of Mr. Roosevelt and billed him as the "World's Greatest Liar."

The Japanese suffered the most from inferiority complex and continually ridiculed and belittled people superior to themselves. They would tell us we were lower than they were since we had raised our hands and surrendered, which was something the enemy had never done in all their 2,600 years of existence. They would always die before disgrace.

"That's fine," I told one of the guards one day. "A good Japanese is a dead Japanese."

He looked at me, confused. He never could understand what that meant.

All prisoners were forced to salute even the lowest private under penalty of punishment. I learned to salute quickly, to bow at the right angle, to keep my eyes down. Survival meant becoming invisible.

The first year in Japan wasn't as bad as the years to follow. But even then, we knew things would get worse. Whenever a prisoner was taken ill or injured, he was taken to the hospital…the stadium. The prisoners knew the place to be a torture-house, or death house. Medicine was one thing that never entered that place. The treatment for all diseases was slow starvation and beatings.

I'd heard the stories from men who'd been there and somehow survived. Self-styled Japanese doctors, who were probably ex-butchers, carried on experiments. Most of the Japanese doctors seemed to be on the borderline of insanity. Prisoners were questioned as to why they had diseases and were told that they should have watched their health more carefully. As sickness, to them, was a form of shirking work, the prisoners would only get half-rations.

The cooks sent up food from the Osaka main camp to the stadium every two days. They sent as much as could be spared and frequently exceeded the ration figures set by the enemy. Sugar was sent up once a month, but the enemy would always appropriate some for themselves.

They'd help themselves to fish and vegetables, and nothing could be done about it.

After six months, some of the men were nothing but skin and bones. Doctor Jackson, surgeon of the Royal Navy, was the prisoners' doctor in charge, and he worked day and night saving as many men as he could. He did some wonderful work, considering the scant amount of medicine and equipment he had access to.

The wooden structures of our bunks were infected with millions of bed bugs and rat fleas from the Japanese soldiers who had occupied them before us. Body lice spread through the camp quickly. Continuous scratching brought on small sores that grew larger. Trying to sleep after a hard day's labor while being tormented all night by insects was its own kind of torture. The bed-bug powder the enemy issued made the bugs fat. The only real solution would have been to burn the place down, and they wouldn't hear of that.

Japanese scientists had published that tea contained vitamin C. This proved true in practice: nearly every man in Osaka drank tea every day, and not one man suffered from pellagra—unlike in the Philippine camps where the disease had been devastating.

Many times he was ordered by the Japanese officers to do certain things that would hurt the men, and he deliberately disobeyed orders. He was severely beaten and kicked as a result, but he never stopped fighting for his patients.

I saw him once, after one of those beatings. His face was swollen, his eye blackened. But he was still standing, still working.

"You all right, Doc?" I asked.

He looked at me and smiled...a tired, grim smile. "I'm fine, lad. Just doing my job."

That was the kind of man Doctor Jackson was. That was the kind of men we all tried to be, in our own ways. We held on. We survived. We waited for the day when we'd be free again.

And we knew, deep down, that day would come. It had to.

| 14 |

Matsumoto

Our first Japanese camp commander was not so bad. He got a little graft, looked the other way when he could, and at least let us have Sundays off. But the second one was terror to all sick men and crippled.

His name was Matsumoto, and I'll never forget the day he arrived at Osaka No. 1. It was early 1943, maybe February or March. The old colonel had been transferred, and we'd heard rumors that the new commander was a hard case. We didn't know the half of it.

Matsumoto was a short, stocky man with a face like carved stone. His orders were that all men would have to work, and this included crippled men not flat on their backs and men partially sick. He stood in the compound that first day and addressed us through Fujimoto.

"New commander say all prisoner must work," Fujimoto translated. "No excuse. If you can stand, you can work."

"What about the sick men?" someone asked.

Fujimoto didn't even bother translating. He just shook his head.

Month after month, Matsumoto tried to set up a work record in man-hours. It became an obsession with him. Sunday had been our one day to wash clothes and scrape together a little rest. Now he grudgingly allowed one day off about once a month, because the only thing that mattered to him was hanging up a new record in working hours.

"We're not men to him," I said to my bunkmate one night. "We're just numbers on a chart."

"Numbers that better keep going up," he replied.

Matsumoto ordered thorough searches at the gate when we returned from work. The ration never covered what a body needed, so men smuggled when they could...eggs, sugar, milk powder, salt. I'd gotten good at it: walk natural with an egg tucked in your armpit, sugar in your shoes, a paper twist of salt under the tongue. But Matsumoto's guards were thorough, and they were brutal.

Whenever something was found, the guard would slap and kick the man, and the duty officer would appear, shouting questions before hauling him to the guardroom for more of the same. Sometimes they made a man kneel on wet rocks for hours.

I saw it happen to a man named Peterson, an Army private from Minnesota. He'd smuggled in three eggs, wrapped in cloth and hidden in his pants. A guard felt the lump.

"Nani?" the guard barked. He smashed the eggs on the ground and started slapping Peterson, hard blows that snapped his head back and forth.

"Where you get? Where you get?"

Peterson tried to answer, but the guard kept hitting. The duty officer arrived, and they dragged Peterson to the guardroom. We heard him yelling for an hour. When they let him out, he could barely walk. His knees were bloody from the rocks, his face swollen and purple.

Under Matsumoto, it got worse.

Smoking in bunk spaces meant a beating. Any time a Japanese officer entered, every prisoner bowed; any hesitation drew a slap or worse. Salutes and bows became weapons...angles, timing, face. He used them to make examples.

I learned to bow quickly, keep my eyes down, move like a shadow.

Some work details took streetcars, packed tight as sardines. Off the cars and onto the march, we could see what civilians were buying. In early 1943 the markets still looked busy, and soldiers had cigarettes.

By late 1943, lines grew longer and shelves thinner. Cigarette rations shrank.

"War's turning," I told my bunkmate.

"How do you figure?"

"Look at what they're eating. Look at what they're smoking."

Black markets had sprung up in Osaka in late 1942. If you had the price, you could find sugar. You could also smell the war in the streets: wood-gas trucks and charcoal burners. A driver would torch a straw bag under the boiler, crank the engine, and belch smoke like a house on fire. From a distance you'd think a block was burning. Up close, it was just a Japanese truck learning to live without gasoline.

The first time I saw one I thought the whole city was going up. The driver cursed, kicked the burner, and finally got it running. Once hot, those rigs hauled big loads. Tires were still around, crude rubber from Sumatra and the islands. Aluminum too…they'd started with deep stocks.

Merchant ships dotted Osaka Bay…scores of them from small coasters to a square-funneled French ship near 20,000 tons tied up at Sumitomo Docks, shuttling between Osaka and Yokohama. Too big for the Japanese to run right, but there she was. A large German freighter came in sometimes; prisoners weren't allowed aboard.

About two hundred POWs worked the docks daily…iron ore, bauxite, cotton, rice, soybeans, salt, wire, steel rails, machinery…anything that kept a war alive.

I was assigned to stevedore work in March 1943. Backbreaking stuff: yo-ho poles biting shoulders, cargo slings, warehouse drags. Still, it got me away from Matsumoto's eyes. Sometimes the honchos gave us a set contract…so many tons of pig iron or bauxite. If we worked smart, we finished early. If we were lucky, we stole food.

Lamp black was the worst cargo, in paper cartons that burst into soot. We'd come back black to the pores, and soap was scarce. The company put out a few bars of fish-oil soap that barely lathered and stank.

Over 25,000 Chinese worked stevedoring in Japan, about 5,000 on ships in Osaka harbor. Some were prisoners, others "volunteers." They unloaded nearly all the coal ships and froze in thin summer clothes and straw sandals, a disgrace.

Many slipped bread and cigarettes to us and shared news from Shanghai. One day in April 1943, a Chinese stevedore handed me a heel of bread and whispered, "Americans win big battle. Many Japanese ship sink."

"Where?"

"Midway. Long time ago. But Japanese never tell truth."

I passed it in camp that night. Old news or not, it meant we were still fighting.

Chinese ship crews sailed under puppet arrangements: a Japanese officer as "captain," with a few ratings to man field guns. POW details that boarded ships searched for caches…overhead beams, storerooms, galleys. Not enough food issued; theft filled the gap.

One day a band of American prisoners removed a storeroom door by pulling the hinge pins, cleared the shelves, and put the door back. When the Japanese cook unlocked it later and saw bare racks, he yelled, then kept his mouth shut. We heard the story and laughed in our sleeves. The crew took the blame.

The most valuable items in camp were sugar, tobacco, and soap. A novel method developed for smuggling alcohol in from the docks: small balloons filled with alcohol, ends secured, placed inside shoulder pads used to carry heavy lumber. A strap sewn to the pad, slung over the shoulder. When the guard searched a man at the gate he would look at the pad and sometimes pinch the ends, but nobody was ever caught that way.

The dock work offered other possibilities. Overloading cargo nets with pig iron could tear chains and collapse booms. Putting a lifting hook into an eye bolt in the lower hold deck and signaling a quick hoist would part a wire cable and give the deck hands hours of repairs while the men in the hold rested. A favorite slogan: Break her—meaning break the winches by overloading. On one occasion the prisoners succeeded in putting a fifteen-hundred-ton ship out of commission for a week.

At Chuba Goon lumberyard, one hour was allowed for lunch. Normally that meant whatever small ration you'd carried from camp—a rice ball and three tiny buns. One day a friend of mine, John Fraft, U.S. Army, suggested we try to catch some of the little garden frogs near a small canal at the end of the yard. Also some small snakes, if we could find them.

Our catch was two small snakes and ten tiny frogs. We cooked them in a metal one-gallon can along with some eggplants appropriated from a Japanese garden nearby. The soup went to our group leader to distribute at noon along with the rice balls.

The point was oil. Snakes and frogs had oil in them, and our bodies needed it. When we couldn't find frogs or snakes, we boiled a plant called sour duck, though too much of it caused diarrhea and you had to calculate how much suffering you could afford.

Under Matsumoto, life in Osaka No. 1 became a grind of work, hunger, and fear. We stole when we could. We helped each other when we could. We survived.

And we watched the war. Rations thinned, smoke rose from ridiculous charcoal trucks, and the guards' eyes changed. The day when the war would turn still felt far away in 1943, but it was coming. We could feel it.

| 15 |

The Boy Corporal

The Boy Corporal earned his nickname from his young face, smooth and unlined like a child's, though his eyes held something old and cruel. Nineteen, maybe twenty, but he carried himself with the swagger of a man who'd discovered power and liked the taste of it.

I first noticed him during morning tenko, standing off to the side with his arms crossed, watching us count off in Japanese. Most of the guards looked bored during roll call, their minds already on breakfast or their next cigarette. Not the Boy Corporal. He watched like a hawk; when someone stumbled, his head tilted a fraction.

"Juu-ichi," I said when my turn came. Eleven.

His eyes flicked to me, then away. I'd gotten it right.

The man three spaces down wasn't so lucky. "Juu... juu-san?" He made it a question, uncertain.

The Boy Corporal moved so fast I barely saw it. One moment he stood by the wall, the next he crossed the space and cracked him across the face. The slap echoed across the compound like a gunshot.

"Again!" he shouted in Japanese. "Zenbu! Hajime kara!" All of you! From the beginning!

We started over. And over. And over. By the sixth time through, my legs were cramping from sitting cross-legged, and the man who'd made the mistake had a welt rising on his cheek like a brand.

That was just the beginning with the Boy Corporal. He had a thing about saluting, an obsession that went beyond even the usual Japanese fanaticism for military courtesy. Every prisoner was required to salute every Japanese soldier, from the colonel down to the lowest private. Even our American officers had to bow and salute to Japanese privates, which burned them worse than the hunger.

But the Boy Corporal took it further. He'd lurk around corners, hide behind buildings, position himself in shadows where you might not see him until it was too late. Then he'd step out, and if you didn't snap to attention fast enough, didn't get your hand up quick enough, didn't hold the salute long enough…well, that was when the fun started. His kind of fun, anyway. We learned to salute doorways, shadows, and our own reflections.

Maloof warned us about him one evening after we'd returned from the docks. "That kid's got a mean streak a mile wide," he said, his voice low. "He's looking for excuses. Don't give him one."

But it was hard not to. We were exhausted, half-starved, our minds fuzzy from malnutrition. Sometimes you'd be so focused on putting one foot in front of the other that you wouldn't notice a guard until you were right on top of him.

That's what happened to Jenkins, a Marine from Wake Island. He was carrying a yo-ho pole loaded with bags of cement, his shoulders screaming, sweat running into his eyes despite the cold. The Boy Corporal stepped out from behind a warehouse just as Jenkins was passing.

Jenkins didn't see him. Didn't salute.

"Kora!" The Boy Corporal's shout made us all freeze. Boots stopped. "You! Stop!"

Jenkins set down the pole, confusion on his face. Then he saw the guard and understood. His hand started to come up in a salute, but it was too late.

The Boy Corporal grabbed him by the collar and dragged him toward the guardroom. We watched, helpless, as Jenkins disappeared inside. We could hear the shouting, the sound of fists on flesh, Jenkins trying not to cry out.

When he came back an hour later, his face was a mess. Both eyes were swelling shut, his lip split, blood crusted under his nose. But that wasn't the worst of it. The Boy Corporal had developed a new technique, something he was proud of.

"He blindfolded me," Jenkins said that night, his words slurred from his swollen mouth. "Put a bandage over my eyes, made me stand at attention. Then he'd hit me. I never knew when it was coming. Sometimes he'd wait a minute, two minutes. Then wham, right in the face. Over and over." He swallowed. "He waits till you breathe easy. Then he hits."

The blindfold became the Boy Corporal's signature. He'd tie it tight, cutting off all light, then circle his victim like a predator. Sometimes he'd whistle. Sometimes he'd click his tongue in the dark…tap, tap…and stay silent long enough for hope to lift before he hit. The not knowing when the blow would come was almost worse than the blow itself.

But even that wasn't enough for him. After a few weeks, he got bored with simple beatings. His mind, twisted as it was, needed something new.

That's when he started with the water.

The first time, it was a British sailor named Hodges who'd failed to salute quickly enough. The Boy Corporal took him to the guardroom as usual, blindfolded him as usual. But this time, instead of just hitting him, he forced Hodges to his knees and shoved his head into a bucket of water. The bucket thudded on the floorboards, water slopping black in the guardroom light.

Hodges came up gasping, choking. Before he could catch his breath, the Boy Corporal pushed him under again. And again. And again.

When Hodges finally stumbled back to the barracks, he couldn't stop shaking. "I thought he was going to drown me," he said, his voice barely a whisper. "I really thought that was it."

The Boy Corporal seemed to feed off our fear. The more we tried to avoid him, the more he sought us out. He'd change his routes, his timing, always trying to catch someone off guard. It became a sick game to him.

One afternoon, I was walking back from Sen Pa Ku with a work detail. We were exhausted, our shoulders aching from unloading bags of rice all day. The Boy Corporal appeared at the camp gate, standing right in the middle of the path.

We all snapped to attention, saluted in unison. But he wasn't satisfied.

"You!" He pointed at Reyes, a kid from Oklahoma who couldn't have been more than twenty-two. "Your salute was slow. Come here."

Reyes's face went white. "Sir, I..."

"Come here!"

Reyes stepped forward. The rest of us stood frozen, watching. The Boy Corporal circled Reyes slowly, like a cat with a mouse. Then, without warning, he kicked Reyes's legs out from under him. Reyes went down hard on the frozen ground.

"Stand up!" the Boy Corporal shouted. "Salute again!"

Reyes struggled to his feet, raised his hand in salute. The Boy Corporal kicked him down again.

"Again!"

This went on for ten minutes. Up, salute, down. Up, salute, down. By the end, Reyes could barely stand. His knees bled through his thin pants, his hands shook so badly he could hardly hold the salute.

Finally, the Boy Corporal waved us away with a disgusted gesture, as if we weren't even worth his time anymore.

That night, Saunders called a meeting of the room leaders. "We need to be extra careful," he said. "That corporal is getting worse. He's looking for any excuse. Make sure your men know...salute early, salute often, and for God's sake, don't give him a reason."

But there was only so much we could do. We were prisoners, powerless, at the mercy of men who saw us as less than human. The Boy

Corporal was just one of many, but he was the worst. His eyes lit up when he had someone at his mercy.

The only thing that kept us going was the knowledge that someday, somehow, this would end. The war couldn't last forever. And when it was over, men like the Boy Corporal would have to answer for what they'd done.

Until then, we endured. We saluted. We bowed. We took the beatings and the humiliations and the torture, and we survived. Because that was all we could do.

Survive.

We saluted the air just to be sure.

| 16 |

The Jail Cell

In the space set aside as a jail…a converted storage room with bars welded across the single window…lodged a POW who was involved in stealing Red Cross cigarettes. The irony wasn't lost on any of us. The enemy stole Red Cross supplies regularly, brazenly, systematically. They got away with it until some fool POW was caught at it, and right away, the enemy found someone to blame for anything that was stolen.

This POW was caught red-handed. His camp had no place to use as a detention room, so he was brought to our camp by a Japanese guard who seemed to take pleasure in shoving the prisoner along with his rifle butt. The man stumbled into the compound, already showing signs of beatings…one eye swollen shut, lip split, knuckles raw.

He was given only half rations. You could see it happening—the hollows deepening under his cheekbones, the way his collar hung off his neck after two weeks, the grey cast his skin took on. His food was measured out in front of him each day, a pitiful amount you could hold in one hand, and he ate it in small careful bites to make it last. He was allowed to go to the W.C. three times a day, no more. The guards kept strict count. If he needed a fourth time, he soiled himself or cramped through it.

He was supposed to do sixty days. We all counted along with him, marking the days in our minds, hoping he'd make it. The man grew thinner, his cheekbones sharp as blades, his eyes sinking into his skull.

But he was tough. He'd been a Marine before Corregidor fell, and Marines don't quit easy.

Then one day, about forty days into his sentence, he managed to get out of his cell. Nobody knew how…maybe the guard got careless, maybe the lock was faulty, maybe desperation gave him strength we didn't know he had. He slipped out during the night and stole some cigarettes from the supply room.

The guards found him in the morning, sitting in his cell, smoking. Just sitting there, drawing on a cigarette like he didn't have a care in the world. Like he'd decided that sixty more days of hell was worth one night of feeling human again.

Another sixty days were added to his sentence. One hundred twenty days total now. Four months in that cell with half rations and three trips to the latrine.

All this time the POW did not have a haircut or a bath. His hair grew long and matted, his beard came in patchy and wild. The smell of him reached us from twenty feet away…the stench of unwashed flesh, of clothes worn day and night for months, of a body slowly consuming itself. When he finally left the camp, he was in a sorry state. We heard he was transferred to another camp, but nobody knew if he made it there alive.

Two American POWs…Bradshaw, a soldier, and Reemer, a Navy man…had been turned in to the Camp Leader by one of the known prisoner of war degenerates for stealing Red Cross parcels. Every camp had them, these men who'd sold their souls for an extra bowl of rice or a cigarette. They informed on their fellow prisoners, curried favor with the guards, did whatever it took to survive another day. We despised them more than we despised the Japanese.

These men, Bradshaw and Reemer, had taken quite a few parcels over the course of several weeks. They'd been staying in the camp, claiming illness, taking it easy while the rest of us worked twelve-hour shifts at the docks or in the factories. They'd gotten comfortable, gotten careless. And someone had noticed.

The Camp Leader, who was a prisoner too...a British Army captain named Thornton...called a session of Kangaroo Court to try these men. We assembled in the compound one evening after work, forming a rough circle around the accused. Thornton stood in the center, his face grave, his uniform as clean as he could manage given our circumstances.

"Bradshaw and Reemer," he said, his voice carrying across the compound, "you stand accused of stealing Red Cross parcels intended for all prisoners. How do you plead?"

Bradshaw, a tall man from Oklahoma with a slow drawl, looked at his feet. "Guilty, sir."

Reemer, shorter and stockier, from somewhere in New Jersey, nodded. "Guilty."

The trial didn't take long. Evidence was presented... testimony from men who'd seen them with extra food, who'd noticed parcels going missing.

"State your name."

"Miller. I saw him with two tins he didn't draw."

"You sure?"

"I counted. One went under his shirt."

Another stepped forward. "Parsons. The parcel list was short three. He was on distribution."

The accused swallowed. "I traded..."

"For whom?" the interpreter snapped.

"For myself."

The verdict was unanimous.

The men were held guilty and sentenced to one month standing night fire watches. They'd get no sleep, just eight hours of standing guard in the cold while the rest of us slept. They lost three months library privileges...not that the library amounted to much, just a few dozen books the Red Cross had sent, but it was something. They lost one meal a day for two days. They worked in the camp every Sunday, which had been our only day of rest. And they carried heavy buckets of rice and soup every day to various rooms in camp, their arms straining under the weight, their backs bent.

It was harsh, but it was fair. We had to police ourselves or we'd tear each other apart. The Japanese wanted us to turn on each other, and we couldn't give them that satisfaction.

But Bradshaw and Reemer did not like this verdict. They talked between themselves in low voices, their heads close together. And then they decided to turn themselves into the enemy, thinking they would get a lighter punishment from the Japanese than from their fellow prisoners.

They failed to reckon with the cruel minds of the Japanese Army.

The morning after they turned themselves in, we watched as they were placed in solitary confinement to await trial. The guards came for them at dawn, dragging them from their bunks, shouting in Japanese. Bradshaw tried to explain, tried to tell them he'd come forward voluntarily, but the guards didn't care. They beat him with their rifle butts until he stopped talking.

Over the following days, we heard the sounds coming from the guardroom. The screams. The pleading. The long silences that were somehow worse than the screaming. They were tortured, slapped, subjected to various humiliations. We learned later that they were forced to sit down on a bench with their feet and hands tied to a stake driven in the ground. They sat like that for hours, their muscles cramping, their circulation cut off, until their hands and feet turned purple and numb.

After two weeks, a court martial was ordered. We watched as they were taken away to a dreaded Military Prison in Osaka, escorted by members of the Kempeitai...the secret police. These were the men even the regular Japanese soldiers feared. They wore plain clothes, carried themselves with an air of absolute authority, and answered only to Tokyo.

Bradshaw could barely walk. His face was a mass of bruises, one arm hung at an odd angle. Reemer was in worse shape...they had to half-carry him to the truck. His eyes were vacant, staring at nothing.

They were never seen again.

Rumors circulated through the camp like wildfire.

"They've got them at Kempeitai," someone whispered in the wash line. "Beating them every few hours."

"Who told you that?"

"Dock detail. Said he heard the screams."

Others swore they were already dead.

"Executed on the second day," a Brit said flatly. "Bullet to the back of the head."

"You saw it?"

"No. But the trucks came back light."

The stories shifted with every meal.

"I heard fingernails," a man muttered over his rice. "Pulled out one by one."

"Shut up," another said. "Save it."

Then, after three months, the word came down, official and cold.

"Bradshaw and Reemer," the interpreter read, "executed for theft of military supplies."

"So that's that," someone said.

"No," I said. "That's the end."

We believed it. We had to. Believing anything else only made the nights longer.

But this later proved false. Years after the war, I learned that both men had survived, though barely. They'd spent the rest of the war in that military prison, subjected to treatment that made our camp look like a resort. Bradshaw lost his arm to gangrene. Reemer lost his mind for a while, though he eventually recovered enough to go home.

The lesson was clear: whatever punishment we prisoners devised for ourselves, it was mercy compared to what the Japanese would do.

What came next only confirmed what we already knew about their nature and their rules.

The average Japanese soldier is a degenerate in some form. I don't say this lightly. I observed them for three and a half years, watched how they treated us, how they treated each other, how they treated their own civilians.

Whenever Japanese soldiers and prisoners of war happened to bathe together...which occurred at the public bathhouse we were sometimes marched to...comments were made by the enemy on how the Americans were so big in body features and how little the Japanese were. They seemed obsessed with it, constantly comparing, constantly measuring. Men and women bathe together and use the same toilets with no concern as to sex in Japan. This was shocking to us Americans at first, though we got used to it.

The guards would stand around naked, pointing at us, laughing, making crude gestures. Some of them seemed genuinely curious, others were clearly trying to humiliate us. We ignored them as best we could, grateful just to have hot water and soap, even if the soap was made from fish oil and barely lathered.

Another form of amusement to the guards was to bring in a prisoner who had broken some rule and place him in the center of a room, slugging and kicking him until he was knocked out. All this took place while he was blindfolded. The prisoner would stand there, hands at his sides, not knowing which direction the next blow would come from. Sometimes five or six guards would participate, circling him like wolves, taking turns.

I saw a man named Patterson endure this once. He'd been caught with a Japanese newspaper, which was strictly forbidden. They blindfolded him and beat him for twenty minutes. When they finally let him go, he couldn't walk straight for a week. His equilibrium was destroyed, his ears ringing constantly.

Another punishment was standing at attention until your legs gave out. You'd start to feel it in your calves first, then the knees, a trembling that worked up through your thighs until your whole lower body was shaking and there was nothing you could do to stop it. When you went down they beat you for not standing. Stand too long and you collapsed. Collapse and you were beaten for collapsing. No exit.

One night a surgeon, Dr. Jackson from H.M.R.N., and two of his assistants had to stand at attention all night for trying to help sick prisoners get Red Cross parcels. From lights out to dawn—eight, nine hours on their feet on cold concrete, hands at their sides, not allowed to lean or shift or sit. By morning their feet had swollen inside their boots. Dr. Jackson was a good man, a skilled surgeon who'd saved dozens of lives with almost no equipment, and they made him stand in the dark for doing his job.

The guards decided this was theft. They made Dr. Jackson and his assistants stand at attention in the compound from 2200 hours until 0600 hours. Eight hours in the cold, not moving, not sitting, not even shifting weight from one foot to the other. By morning, Dr. Jackson's legs were swollen to twice their normal size. He could barely walk for three days.

The enemy would hurt, punish, and humiliate the Americans in every way they could. It wasn't random cruelty...it was policy, handed down from the top.

The Japanese Headquarters' Commander, who was a Colonel, told the prisoners in a speech through an interpreter that all prisoners of war would receive treatment borderline between human and inhuman.

He said it plainly, without shame, without apology. We would be kept alive, but barely. We would be fed, but not enough. We would be given shelter, but not comfort. We would be treated as less than human, because in their eyes, that's what we were.

We were men who had surrendered. We had chosen life over death, and in the Japanese military code, that made us contemptible. Unworthy of respect. Unworthy of mercy.

The Colonel's words stayed with me through all the months that followed. Whenever I wondered if things could get worse, I remembered: borderline between human and inhuman. That was the promise. That was the policy.

And they kept their promise.

| 17 |

Mostly Inhuman

As it turned out, the treatment was mostly inhuman. The Colonel's promise...borderline between human and inhuman...was a lie. There was no borderline. Only cruelty, systematic and deliberate.

Guards slapped and kicked prisoners for sport. A man could be walking in the compound and, for no reason beyond a passing whim, take a backhand to the mouth. The crack of palm on cheek, the copper taste of blood, the hum in the ears...it became part of the soundscape.

The real mover sat under all of it: an inferiority that needed us on our knees. Every slap and bow drill said the same thing...We conquered you. You are nothing.

The English caught it a shade less than we did. Not mercy...math. The planes over Osaka at night were American. The fires were American. The grief the civilians talked about in the lines the next morning was laid at our feet. They took it out on us with venom.

When the Sumitomo sirens started, the wail climbed the spine of the city. Lights went dead on command. Silence. Guards posted at exits, rifles ready, orders clear: try to slip out in the confusion and you're shot.

We sweated out the raids in blackness, listening to the engines gather like a storm front. Over our camp the B-29s felt impossibly high...sound like an express train rolling the roof. Then the bombs. The sky blinked white, then red, noon for a heartbeat and back to night. Flak stitched upward, tracers beading like red rosaries that touched nothing. The ground lifts, the lungs empty, dust sifts down from rafters, men pray, men curse, men go quiet. You learn the whistle code: high is far; low is close; no whistle at all means it's already yours.

One night a blast rocked the barracks and I fell fifteen feet from the top rack. Hit the corner of a mess table and then the floor. In the dark, it sounded like a bomb had come through. Someone risked a match…you weren't supposed to…and there I was, breathless on the concrete.

In the morning, Lieutenant Hoffman, U.S. Army, examined me. No bones broken. Shock and bruises. Lucky, he said.

I was luckier than I knew. The fall put me on light duty for two weeks. A transfer picked twenty men to a camp near Kyoto…bad place by every whisper. Swamps to fill, ditches to dig, loads on the back, starvation for seasoning. Men there three months lost ten to fifty pounds. Some didn't come back. I would have been number twenty-one. A sailor named Kowalski went instead. I never saw him again. Later I heard Kyoto killed him.

Most mornings ran on a wire. At 0500 a rifle butt on the door: Okiro. By 0525, washed, dressed, in place for tenko. Sit cross-legged, count off in Japanese. One error and the whole line starts again. The man who fumbled the numbers drew the slap or the guardroom.

After roll call, asa meshi. Three-fifty grams of rice, about two hundred grams of green-top soup salted thin, sometimes a smear of soya paste. Under or overcooked…never right. We ate standing or squatting, wooden spoons we'd whittled, five minutes to swallow and stack bowls.

"All hands!" at 0640. Working parties out the gate at the double, salutes ready. If the commander stood there, hands behind his back, he expected perfection. Miss it, and you were marked for the day. I saw a Marine named Henderson shuffle sick past the gate one morning. The commander stepped in, slapped him spinning, then kicked him in the ribs. Guardroom swallowed him for three days.

In the street the honchos counted heads for factories and docks. Illiterate, mean, and eager for favor, they'd been told to grind us and report names. Orders came in Japanese; the interpreter passed them along like he enjoyed it. March distances varied...some details walked thirty minutes; a few took streetcars packed with civilians who stared like we were another species.

Work was a catalogue of weights. Ashes, coal, sand, bricks on the yo-ho pole...two men under a long spar with baskets in the middle, seventy kilos, a hundred fifty-four pounds. The pole bit the collarbone and chewed a permanent callus into the shoulder. Miss a step and the balance dumped you. I carried coal to a warehouse for three months and still feel the pad of scar to this day.

Other jobs scalded or poisoned you. Foundries poured heat into the lungs until men coughed blood. Chemical plants burned airways raw. The docks ran in sleet, rain, and August glare. We were expected to match healthy laborers on starvation fuel. Fall behind, and boots and rifle butts fixed the pace. Fall down, and they kicked you up. Die, and your ashes went home in a box.

This was the routine. Years condensed to a clock and a bowl and the ache in the legs. We endured because there wasn't a second option. Somewhere under the hunger we held to a thin wire of belief...that America would win, that we'd step out of this gate as free men, that a morning would come without sirens. And it did, but not before the city burned and a generation of nights turned into one long noise.

| 18 |

Fire from the Sky

By 1944, the Japanese militarists were working day and night to exhort the people into a greater war effort. Rations were being continually cut. American submarines were constantly cutting shipments into Japan. With the fall of the Philippines, the order was given to all Japanese people that they must produce and work harder than ever before. The Americans must be stopped at all costs.

The enemy's desperation showed in everything they did. Guards became more brutal. Work quotas increased. Food rations shrank. The Japanese people themselves were suffering, their faces growing gaunt, their clothes more ragged with each passing month. Black market prices soared to insane levels...500 yen for a pair of shoes, 1,000 yen for a bicycle, 70 yen per pound for sugar. The pre-war value of the yen had been 3.35 to every U.S. dollar. Now it was worthless paper backed by a crumbling empire.

We prisoners watched it all with grim satisfaction. Every cut in rations, every desperate order from Tokyo, every haggard face on the street told us the same story: Japan was losing. The question wasn't if anymore, but when.

There were no air raid shelters provided for the sick prisoners lodged in Ichi Oki, the stadium where the enemy formerly had track meets and baseball games. Underneath the bleachers, concrete spaces had been divided into bunk spaces for sick prisoners. Raised partitions made of wood were built up from the deck about two feet, and coarse straw was scattered around to sleep on. About 125 patients were kept here suffering from various diseases...beriberi, dysentery, malaria, malnutrition, and a dozen other ailments that came from three years of starvation and brutality.

The routine was hell. All prisoners who were not bed patients had to keep out of their bunks during the day. There was no recreation whatsoever. All Japanese had to be saluted. The messing situation was half-rations to all men. Breakfast consisted of one small bowl of cooked barley and water. Three tiny buns, about 150 grams in weight, and weak Japanese tea without milk or sugar were issued for lunch. Supper was cooked rice and vegetable soup, about half a pint made with daikon...radishes...or some sort of greens.

This diet was slowly killing the sick patients off day by day. Some of the things prisoners would do to lessen the pangs of hunger were to save all tea leaves and put them into their watery soup and eat them. One American prisoner had some dry fish powder sent to the stadium by a friend. He would take his three buns and shred them up, then mix in a little fish powder and roll them into little pellets. After finishing this task, he would slowly eat the pellets, taking several hours or more, making each tiny morsel last.

Conversation centered on food and recipes all day. A man describing his mother's pot roast while your stomach was a fist of nothing—that was the daily texture of it. You'd hear a man across the barracks talking about apple pie, the smell of cinnamon, the crust his wife made, and your mouth would fill with spit you had nothing to spend it on. It was its own kind of torture. It was also the only thing that made the hours move.

The sick prisoners underwent tragic and inhuman conditions. The Japanese motto for a sick man was "He who does not work need not have as much food as they who work all day." The enemy figured the more prisoners who died, the less they would have to feed. They knew one of the men's thoughts was to try and keep alive for the day when they would be freed and could return to their loved ones. If the enemy could prevent this, they would feel good considering the sorrow caused to the prisoners' relatives when they found their loved one was dead.

My opinion of the enemy is that they do not have a shred of decency or feeling for any human being. The average Japanese has an inferiority complex, cruel nature, short temper, and ignorance of human rights.

Then came March 13, 1945.

The sirens atop the five-story Sumitomo building started wailing around 10:00 p.m. We'd heard them before...dozens of times. But this time felt different. The sound went on and on, rising and falling like a wounded animal. Lights were immediately put out. The word was passed for complete silence. If anybody attempted to escape, they would be shot.

In pitch-black darkness we waited. Over our camp the B-29s seemed to fly at a very high altitude with a terrible noise like an express train. The sound built and built until it filled the world. Then came the bombs.

Down they came...the whole sky lighting up amid anti-aircraft and machine-gun fire. We died a thousand deaths waiting for a bomb to strike the camp, which was very close to the waterfront. The building shook. Dust rained down from the ceiling. Men prayed in the darkness, some out loud, some silently.

The raid struck Osaka and continued for twenty-seven hours. Twenty-seven hours of hell. One-third of the city was afire. From our barrack's windows we were able to see the mighty armada in its magnificent display of strength and force. Wave after wave of B-29s, their silver bodies catching the light of the fires below. The Japanese put up a fighter defense but these planes could not reach the altitude of the B-29s. Few, if any, B-29s were shot down.

The water system suffered heavy damage, as did the power system. The enemy was well impressed. So were we. Our morale was steadily going up while the average Japanese's morale was fast going down.

We stayed in camp three days during which we could not see the damage done and also could avoid any attacks by the Japanese civilians. When we finally went back to work, we quickly surveyed the damage. All the prisoners were well impressed and amazed. Entire city blocks were gone…just ashes and twisted metal. The Osaka street car barns had been hit and they were just charred and twisted wrecks.

Devastating raids were carried out by the B-29s and B-25s from March 1944 to June 1, 1945. Each raid was bigger than the last. Each raid brought us closer to freedom.

Then came June 1, 1945.

The raid that put the clincher on Osaka.

It started just after dark. The sirens wailed. We scrambled to our positions, knowing the drill by now. But this time was different. This time the enemy came in force…an armada estimated by the prisoners to be from 740 to 2,000 planes. The sky was black with them.

The bombs fell like rain. Fire bombs, mostly…incendiaries that burst into white-hot flames on contact. The camp quickly caught fire despite the efforts of all the prisoners and Japanese. Within thirty minutes, the camp burnt to the ground.

Before the air raid, nearly all the prisoners had been sent out to the various companies, which undoubtedly saved many lives. Only about one hundred men were in camp. A few were injured. None killed. It was a miracle.

The gallant camp galley staff worked in the big brick warehouse across from the camp, stowing bags of rice even as the bombs fell around them. These men, both American and English, led by Dix, Quartermaster sergeant, worked to save the foodstuffs. All during the fire and bombings, they never stopped. As soon as the bombing was over, they managed to have a truck brought up to the warehouse doors. Many hundreds of bags of rice, beans, sugar and other foods were saved.

The Japanese colonel sent word that unless all rice and foods were saved, all prisoners would probably be without food, as nearly all of the Japanese government warehouses were bombed out. For once, the enemy needed us more than we needed them.

All camp staff men and some men who had various illnesses were put to work salvaging everything they could, including medical and clothing supplies. About 60% of the entire camp supplies were saved. Hardly any personal clothing or valuables belonging to prisoners who were out at work were saved. This constituted a great loss as many men were wearing wooden clogs to work and leaving their shoes in camp.

A funny thing happened during the raid. The burning of the camp roasted a pig, some rabbits and chickens that belonged to the Japanese staff soldiers. Had they been saved, no doubt the enemy would have eaten them, but as they did burn, their carcasses were given to the Americans and we had the benefit of burnt meat soup. It was the first meat we'd had in months.

The enemy would not issue any clothing. Their main reason was lack of transportation to areas not bombed out. Also with the loss of the camp, the American and British prisoners might be transferred to some other area and the Osaka Military would not be liable for any further keeping of clothing.

Rumors were that all prisoners would be transferred to some small island near Mojie or Tokyo. However, on June 2, 1945, all prisoners, amounting to 500 or more, were moved into a filthy ex-Chinese coolie barracks that also had formerly been a British prisoners' camp. Here, 500 men would be crowded into a two-story building which could only accommodate 150, or less. Bedbugs, lice and filth were prevalent all over. All water and food was strictly rationed.

Directly across from the old building was the huge Sumitomo warehouse…four stories of reinforced concrete. Outside in their yard space were stacks of tin bars, copper and tungstite metals. During the night, these bars glowed due to the heat produced by the fires started by the B-29s. The bombing of Sumitomo warehouses was very disastrous and many tons of sugar and rice were lost. The warehouses were made of brick with wooden roofs and these roofs quickly burned down. The steel in the buildings got so hot that there was just a mass of buckled girders.

After the bombing, any person could see for at least two miles or more the vast burned spaces. The city of Osaka was fast taking on the picture of desolation and ruin. Japanese civilians' and soldiers' morale was going down quickly. Food was becoming very scarce. Salt was becoming scarcer every day. Bandages and medicines were unobtainable.

All during the time we were inside the old building, the cook staff, headed by Quartermaster Sergeant Dix, Wells, a first class baker, and Egan, Ship's cook, did a wonderful job getting food prepared for the hungry men. It was about twelve hours after the bombing of Osaka before any prisoner received any food due to the lack of facilities to cook food. Most of the cooking gear was burned and warped. The Japanese people were very jittery and fully expected the B-29 raids to continue for many days.

Our camp interpreter, who went by the name of Hayashi and could speak English very well, got very tough after the bombing. He slapped a few men around and issued very stern and forceful orders. Although Hayashi did a lot of good for all prisoners, he was under constant pressure and surveillance by the Japanese Army Camp Staff. Any Japanese who could speak English was always under suspicion that he might show too friendly an attitude to the prisoners. Our camp interpreter had been General Motors representative in Hawaii for ten years and fully understood American feelings and rights. On the whole, relations between the interpreter and the prisoners progressed very well.

Our prison camp commander, Saunders, CBM, U.S. Navy, who was captured at Guam, also did an excellent job conducting the affairs and relations between the Japanese and the prisoners. Another man who really was a tremendous help in working conditions and clothing for prisoners was Maloof, BM, 1st class, U.S. Navy. He was never afraid of the enemy and was well respected and liked by all prisoners and Japanese alike.

The Japanese camp commander, Colonel Murata, was continually demanding more work from all the prisoners under threats of food cuts. His stooge, sub-lieutenant Matsumoto, used many ideas of his own, probably without the camp commander's knowledge, and struck or kicked any prisoners who would disobey orders or cause any trouble. His features resembled those of the small tree-monkey.

The raid of June 1, 1945, destroyed many warehouses of a trading company called Kurahasi, containing bran, rice, sugar, metals, sweet potatoes, and more. One of their large waterfront warehouses contained 25,000 cases of canned tangerines, which were held for emergency rations. Sumitomo, exporters of Osaka, Japan, lost 50,000 bags...weighing 100 kilos each...of sugar, ear-marked to become alcohol for fuel. They also lost expensive machinery, electrical motors, and mechanical equipment, but their large four-story building suffered only minor damage.

The Japanese civilians were looting any food or valuables they could and the Kempeitai had their hands full trying to cope with the civilians. The Osaka street railway system was nearly wiped out and only a few streetcars escaped damage. This bombing of the railway system was a serious blow to the enemy as thousands of people used the railway system as their sole means of getting to and from work. Some of the cars, ten to fifteen blocks from the car barns, were observed to be a mess of twisted metal, as if the falling incendiary bombs had hit them by chance.

All Japanese expected invasion in September or October 1945. Japanese soldiers were working day and night loading troop transports for voyage to Kyushu, as there were many rumors to the effect that landings would be made in southern Japan. Rations of tobacco and fuel and foods lowered every day.

On July 2, 1945, an accident happened to Willie Cronin, Chief Torpedoman, U.S. Navy Reserve. He was stooping down picking up red beans that had mixed into a cargo of soya beans when a cargo boom swung out above him. Two bags of beans, weighing 104 kilos each, came down on him. It broke both ankles, his back, and his nose, and paralyzed him.

He was still conscious when they brought him back to camp. That evening he said to the pharmacist's mate and anyone nearby: "Well, doc, guess I'll keep the fellows up tonight, although I feel okay. Funny thing—I can't seem to move a muscle in my body."

Willie Cronin was a Navy pensioner who had been called back to duty after hostilities broke out. He was married. He had four children.

On the night of August 1, 1945, we felt it before we heard it—a low vibration in the floor, in the walls, in your back teeth. Then the sound arrived: a deep continuous thunder rolling in from the south, and the sky in that direction went orange. Three or four hundred B-29s, we'd learn later, hitting Japanese and Korean barracks ten miles away. For ten hours the horizon burned. The ground trembled with each wave. We lay in our bunks and listened and didn't say anything and about seven thousand men died in the firelight we watched from the camp.

The next day our interpreter told us about the raid and said the American fliers had killed hundreds of women and children—which was the standard Japanese excuse for every raid. When Japanese bombers killed women and children, that was another matter. They were doing it for the Emperor.

It was regrettable that only two atom bombs were dropped on Japan.

We watched it all from our filthy barracks. We watched the city burn. We watched the enemy scramble. We watched their empire crumble.

And we knew...we all knew...that the end was coming soon.

On June 5 barges transferred all American prisoners to another camp called Omori, surrounded by dock installations and heavy industry, no air-raid shelters provided. On June 29 a train moved us again to Nagoya Camp Number Ten—coal storage bins converted to makeshift barracks, small-gauge coal car tracks pulled up and covered with dirt.

A considerable number of Dutch prisoners were also at Nagoya Ten. Most of them were unable to work—old age, sickness, or pure refusal. The interpreter laughed whenever anyone complained about food. He said all prisoners were no good.

| 19 |

Freedom

The morning of August 16, 1945, 294 prisoners were at work loading coal aboard railroad cars, when at 08:15 a.m. the Japanese honchos (foremen) were observed bowing towards the sun and mumbling some kind of gibberish. I kept my head down, shoveling coal into the straw bags like I'd done a thousand times before. The coal dust coated my throat, my lungs, every inch of exposed skin. But something felt different.

Suddenly, they shouted in the Japanese language, "Work finished...go back to prisoner camp!"

I straightened up, my back screaming in protest. Around me, other men stopped mid-motion, coal shovels frozen in their hands. We looked at each other, not daring to believe what we'd just heard.

"What the hell?" someone muttered.

The cars were only loaded about one fifth full and here it was only 08:15 when work started at 07:00 a.m. In three years and four months, the Japanese had never stopped work early. Never. They'd worked us through air raids, through typhoons, through men collapsing from exhaustion and starvation. They'd worked us until we dropped.

"Possible, the war is over," I said to the man next to me, a Marine from Guam whose name I'd never learned.

"If this were only true," he whispered back.

Maybe some monkey general was going to make a speech. Maybe the enemy had searched the camp and found something to make them good and angry. Maybe they were going to line us all up and shoot us. After three years of captivity, you learned not to hope too hard. Hope could kill you faster than starvation.

Some of the Japanese work bosses approached us, their faces unreadable. One of them, a honcho who'd beaten me twice for working too slowly, said in broken English, "You not come back to work any more."

The words hung in the air like smoke.

"Any more?" someone repeated.

"War finish," the honcho said, then turned away.

We knew then. The war must surely be over.

For a moment, nobody moved. Then, like a dam breaking, men scattered in every direction. Many of the men quickly went to places they had rice, beans, and other food hidden and retrieved them to take back into camp. I'd stashed a small bag of rice behind some lumber three weeks ago, and I went for it now, moving fast despite my weakened legs. Even if the war was over we still were under the rule of the Army militarist. We'd learned the hard way that the Japanese could change their minds about anything.

The march back to camp felt surreal. The guards walked alongside us, but they didn't kick anyone. They didn't shout. They just walked, their rifles slung over their shoulders, their eyes on the ground.

The days spent in camp were long days of waiting, thinking and wondering what would happen next. Will American troops rescue us, or will the enemy take us to some ship and transfer us to a repatriation center? The uncertainty gnawed at us worse than hunger. We'd survived this long. We couldn't die now, not when freedom was so close we could almost taste it.

Many wild rumors were going around the camp. One rumor was that the American Red Cross or Switzerland representatives would call at the camps and get our names and find out whether any of the men were sick. Another rumor said the Japanese were going to march us into the mountains and execute us all before the Americans arrived. That one kept me awake at night.

Red Cross officials came into camp the 29th of August 1945. They were the first white men we'd seen in over three years who weren't prisoners. They wore clean clothes. Their faces were full, their eyes clear. They looked at us like we were ghosts, and maybe we were. We all thought that since the war is now over, we ought to get plenty of food, but we did not, until continual arguments and complaints were made to the camp commandant and little by little, a small amount of food was issued in addition to our regular ration.

The enemy objection was that there was no rice or vegetables available, which was a lie, as warehouses were full. Even with defeat, the enemy was still trying to rule and make things difficult for American prisoners. Some things never changed.

Then came the news that changed everything.

A radio dispatch was received by the camp commandant to the effect to notify prisoner camp leaders to erect a large Prisoner of War sign on top of the roofs of their barracks so B-25's and other planes would drop food by parachutes.

We painted the letters ten feet high using whatever we could find. POW. Three letters that meant salvation.

This was joyous news after existing on inferior Japanese food for so long. August 28, 1945, made the 8th day since we had quit work and the days were really long. Time moved differently now. Before, the days had blurred together in an endless cycle of work, hunger, and sleep. Now, every hour dragged. We were being issued Japanese clothing, khaki Japanese Army shoes, and other supplies. One month ago, pleas were sent in to the camp commandant to issue clothing and shoes to prisoners who were working at various jobs without shoes or with ragged clothing. The answer was always that the Japanese had no clothes to issue, and maybe they could in the near future.

Now the war was over, and the enemy would probably issue enough clothes and blankets to last a lifetime. The irony wasn't lost on any of us.

On the 2nd of September, 1945, about 10:00 a.m. a radio was brought in, which was the first one in three years and some odd months. We were to listen to a speech to be made by General MacArthur, but as usual, the Japanese manufactured radio failed to function and we were left in the dark. Some of the men cursed. Others laughed. After everything we'd been through, of course the radio wouldn't work.

At 10:45 a.m. September 2, 1945, American Marines and soldiers proceeded to the camp gate and there, the Japanese guards surrendered their rifles to our men.

I was standing in the compound when it happened. I watched those guards...men who'd beaten us, starved us, worked us half to death...hand over their weapons to American soldiers. The Marines were young, well-fed, their uniforms crisp and clean. They looked at us with shock and pity.

This was a gala day after three years and four months as prisoners of war.

If only we could lock up all the Japanese guards and officials until American soldiers arrived by plane. The thought crossed every man's mind. But our camp leader called a meeting and all prisoners fell out into the court and there we were read the U.S. Navy regulations pertaining to the laws for the good of the U.S. Navy. Any prisoners must take on no violence or any other forms of punishment against the enemy.

It was the right thing to do, but it was hard. Real hard.

Colonel E. A. Johnson, U.S. Army, had parachuted into our camp and informed us that Red Cross supplies would be dropped into our camp sometime between September 1 and 5. We also would be transported to an airfield about five miles from our camp and be flown out of Japan.

We were getting happier every day with all this good news.

Today, at approximately 09:45 a.m. September 4, 1945, one large type U.S. Navy plane came over our camp and dropped ninety-five parachutes holding four cases each of U.S. Army menu-type rations. The parachutes bloomed in the sky like flowers, white against the blue. Men cheered and wept. They were retrieved from the rice patches and some from the camp. We now would have enough food to hold us until the American forces rescued us.

I opened my first case with shaking hands. Inside were cans of meat, crackers, chocolate, cigarettes, matches. I held a Hershey bar and just stared at it. Three years and four months since I'd seen one.

Several U.S. Army officers who had made the trip to our camp from Headquarters in Nagoya gave us some information. They came into our camp about 12:00 midnight and most of the prisoners got up to look at these officers, as they were the first American white men we had seen or talked to in over three years. They certainly made us feel good.

All the cigarettes the officers had, they gave to the prisoners and told us not to worry as efforts were being made to get us out of camp as soon as possible. We were told that Colonel E.A. Johnson was negotiating with the proper authorities to have us flown from Nagoya to Tokyo or Manila.

We were all highly in favor of this plan as we were anxious to get back to the good old American shores and see our loved ones again. We also wanted to get acquainted with our various service organizations. We were also told that Colonel E. A. Johnson had shot down twenty-four Nip planes and we all thought he was a great fighter and pilot.

The enemy in Nagoya Camp Headquarters was disappointed because they had lost the war and were jealous of all the Red Cross food we were getting. Hundreds of Chinese and Koreans were forming lines outside the camp to receive any food we might give them. Even Japanese were clamoring for food. It was a wonderful feeling to have all the food you wanted after being starved for three years and four months.

I can truthfully say those prisoners who had faith and the courage to wait were now reaping their reward. Those who were weak and couldn't stand the gaff went down, never to rise again. I thought of the men who'd died in the stadium, in the holds of the *Totoru Maru*, on the work details. They'd been so close.

September 5, about 6:00 p.m. all the prisoners were escorted by Kempeitai secret police to waiting railroad coaches for the journey to Yokohama, where U.S. Naval forces would meet us.

For the first time, prisoners were to ride railroad cars without having to have the blinds drawn down. I pressed my face against the window and watched Japan roll past. The next day, all we could see was desolation caused by the American air raid over Japan. Every hamlet and city was damaged. Some burnt, others just twisted steel girders, which was all that remained of some industries.

The destruction was total. Complete. I felt no pity.

On the way, all prisoners had all the K-rations they wanted and we were feeling good. Only one thing upset most prisoners. It was the orange and lemon powders to mix with the water as we drank it, it made our tongues sore because we were not accustomed to so much acid. Our bodies had been starved for so long that even good food hurt.

A total of twenty hours were spent aboard the railroad cars and they were very uncomfortable, being so hot in the daytime and so cold at night. The train went through a very long tunnel and all the prisoners were covered with black soot.

In a small town going towards Yokohama some American planes were sighted flying at low altitude. All the prisoners started waving like mad. The American planes immediately dived down and flew over the train several times. The roar of their engines was the most beautiful sound I'd ever heard.

Finally, the leader plane dropped a message. The message read, "Do you need food? Will drop some, answer by means of signs, yes or no."

We all had strips of parachute material from Red Cross parachutes given to us for souvenirs and the letters "NO" were formed as an answer.

Then a swell air show was staged for us. The little planes would dive down to the train and zoom up with a loud noise. We were all very thrilled and excited. They were showing off for us, and we loved every second of it.

Finally, our train signaled time to proceed and we all climbed back aboard for the trip back to Yokohama and Freedom.

On the 6th of September 1945, our railroad trip ended. We arrived at a small town about 22 miles from Yokohama, where we were met by U.S. Navy officers and enlisted men who welcomed us back to the protection of the United States flag. We were given hot tea, served by the Japanese porters and then the word was passed for us to throw our lice-infested clothes in one pile and to take as little as possible of our possessions to the U.S. Navy hospital ship, USS *Rescue*.

I stripped off the rags I'd worn for months and threw them on the pile without a second thought. After disposing of our meager possessions, small trucks were waiting to take groups of six men down to the temporary docks where American powerboats, landing types, were standing by.

An American officer was at the top of the large stone steps bawling out orders for boat coxswains to take the ex-prisoners aboard and convey them to the USS *Rescue*. As the breakers were heavy, the coxswain ran at reduced speed on the trip out. The hospital ship could be made out and before long the powerboat drew alongside.

Quickly, the ex-prisoners scrambled up the ladder to be met by various Navy men who directed them to place their possessions in one pile as they would have to check our gear for possible vermin.

In the fantail, port side, all the ex-P.O.W's. were walking around waiting to go down below to receive a thorough shower, medical inspection and new American clothing. What a wonderful feeling it was to once more be clean and have white man's clothing.

The shower was hot. I stood under it for twenty minutes, watching three years of filth wash away. The water ran black at first, then brown, then finally clear. A Navy corpsman handed me soap...real soap...and I scrubbed until my skin was raw.

All the ex-prisoners were issued new shoes and I was given a pair of Navy low shoes, size 9½ EE. My size was 7½ D but I didn't kick because they felt good even if they were too large. My dungarees fitted well around the waist except they were too long in the legs, which I rolled up. I looked ridiculous, but I didn't care. They were American dungarees.

Our first official Navy meal came about 12:00 and it consisted of fruit Jell-O, meat loaf, fried potatoes, sliced tomatoes, cake, sliced bread, fresh milk, butter and coffee. We would have any amount we could eat and all the prisoners were thankful that once more food would be plentiful without having to exist on a starvation diet.

I ate slowly, forcing myself not to gorge. Men around me were crying as they ate. The meat loaf tasted like heaven. The bread was soft and white. The milk was cold and sweet. I'd dreamed of this meal for three years and four months, and now it was real.

We were free.

We were going home.

Forty-eight of us were transferred to an American APD—a fast destroyer transport—for the voyage to a rendezvous point about two hundred miles from Tokyo. Bunks assigned, mess call sounded at 1700, movies on the starboard quarterdeck afterward. It was the first time in three years and four months that I had the privilege to see and hear something only the United States could produce. I watched the screen and couldn't stop smiling.

In the morning the APD got underway. At the rendezvous we transferred to an Australian destroyer, the H.M.A.S. Warramunga. The Australians went out of their way to make us comfortable. Movies every night, hundreds of magazines and books, extra portions whenever you wanted them. The food was excellent. Two hundred miles to Tokyo, and we enjoyed every one of them.

As we approached Tokyo Bay, warships appeared on all sides—American, British, Australian. Battleships. Carriers. Ships none of us had ever seen. We stood on deck and stared. Three years ago we had watched our Navy die in Manila Bay. Now this.

Inside the harbor, hundreds of logs drifted across the water, hazards set loose to damage small craft. The breakwater buoys were painted with the name of the first American ship to enter Tokyo harbor.

A motor launch took us ashore to a small dock. Transportation was waiting to drive us twenty-two miles southeast to a Japanese airfield called Kisarazi. About seventy or eighty Japanese fighter planes sat grounded on the field, rendered useless by American Navy men. Piles of Japanese rifles and aircraft parts lay in the open. Some of the men wanted souvenirs. Others wanted nothing to do with any of it.

Word came that twenty-two of us would board a DC-54 for Guam that evening. We signed forms certifying we were flying by our own decision and were not forced to. The big doors closed. We were airborne, the field lights blinking below us.

The plane circled three times and the men were beginning to think something was wrong. Something was wrong. The running lights had failed and the pilot captain decided to return to the field rather than risk a night approach somewhere else. An excellent landing. We went to the operations office and had a cup of coffee. Cots had been set up in the hangar. We turned in.

After breakfast the next morning we were airborne again, bound for Guam at two hundred miles per hour, eight thousand nine hundred feet. We landed at 1725.

Naval transportation took us to Quonset huts set aside as hospital quarters. We answered forms about our activities as prisoners and about Japanese war criminals. Then the mess hall—excellent food. Then the American Red Cross, which issued each man a Comfort Kit: cigarettes, cookies, candy, gum, soap. Free cablegrams. Most men either turned in early or went to the movies, which were shown outdoors.

Guam had changed. The small naval station I remembered from before the war had become one of the largest bases in the Pacific—miles of concrete highways, massive installations, the biggest airfield I'd ever seen. Japanese soldiers were still hiding in the hills, ambushing Marines, and search parties were going out after them. Even here, the war wasn't quite finished with everyone.

Next stop was Kwajalein, Marshall Islands. The pilot let each man come up to the cockpit and sit in the co-pilot's seat. Looking down from nine thousand feet, I watched a ship crossing below us. It looked small. I kept thinking about Corregidor, about Japanese bombers flying at twenty-five thousand feet, and what we must have looked like to them.

We landed at Kwajalein just after 2000. Transportation to the Red Cross hut, where every comfort was on offer. The Navy mess if you were hungry. Free beer if you wanted it. After three years and four months, I had one and it tasted like the world.

The crew rigged bunks on the aircraft for the long run to Pearl Harbor. I was nearly thrown from my top bunk when the plane hit an air pocket. I lay there in the dark over the Pacific and thought that was probably the least dangerous thing that had happened to me in four years.

John Rodgers airfield at Pearl Harbor. Transportation to Aiea Heights for medical checkups. The Naval Relief issued clothing to anyone who needed it—dungarees, underwear, white hats, shoes. The Marine Corps issued khakis, a cap, belt, field jacket. We were pronounced medically fit.

Then a DC-47 to Alameda, California, arriving September 12, 1945. A bus to Oakland-Knoll Naval Hospital, and small barracks arranged for us. Most of the men went straight into Oakland to celebrate.

| 20 |

Coming Home

The food ordered by the men at Oakland-Knoll hospital was a luxury beyond anything we'd imagined during those years in Japan. I ordered waffles with fresh whipped cream, fresh strawberries and ice cream. After trying one of these delectable treats, I decided another one would be in order and I soon became full. Some of the men ordered full fried chickens, T-bone steaks, porterhouse steaks and a host of other foods. Very little drinking was in evidence. We were too focused on food, on the simple pleasure of eating without fear, without rationing, without the gnawing hunger that had been our constant companion.

Quite a few men had relatives to visit. Some had their wives in Oakland and were trying to readjust themselves to the lives of people who were civilized and not slaves to a militarist cause. The adjustment wasn't easy. We'd spent so long being beaten down, being told we were lower than dirt, that it felt strange to walk freely, to speak without fear of a slap or a kick.

What a thrill it was to talk to my wife, Jeanette. My call came from Oakland, California, and hers was all the way from Auburn, New York. Her voice came over the phone clearly and undistracted. For the first time in nearly six years, I was able to talk and hear my wife's voice. I could barely speak at first. The words caught in my throat. She was crying, and I found myself crying too, something I hadn't allowed myself to do in all those years as a prisoner.

"Frank?" she said, her voice breaking. "Is it really you?"

"It's me, Jeannie," I managed. "I'm coming home."

She told me about Valerie, our daughter I'd never met. Six years old now. She'd been born while I was on Corregidor, and I'd only seen photographs. Jeanette described her dark hair, her bright eyes, how she asked about her daddy every night. The girl had grown up with a ghost for a father, a man in a photograph who existed somewhere far away in a war she couldn't understand.

"She's so excited to meet you," Jeanette said. "She's been practicing what she'll say."

I didn't know what to say to that. How do you meet your own daughter for the first time when she's six years old? What do you say to a child who's been waiting her whole life for a father she's never known?

By the time six days had elapsed, I was scheduled to leave Alameda Air Base on September 18, 1945. The first stopover would be Winslow, Arizona. After having my baggage weighed...we were allowed 45 pounds...I boarded a DC 47 for the trip across the country. I viewed some wonderful scenery passing over California, brown desert country and high dunes. The landscape was so different from the cramped holds of the *Totoru Maru*, from the bombed-out ruins of Osaka, from the gray walls of the prison camp.

We arrived at our first stop, which was Winslow, Arizona, but we only stopped a few hours and were off again for Kansas City, Missouri. Here, the Red Cross was on the job and all food was free. I ate slowly, savoring every bite, still not quite believing that I could have as much as I wanted. At Columbus, Ohio, our third stopover, a very nice little airport was observed. There, Red Cross ladies quickly invited us to all the food we wanted including ice cream, free.

My brother lived in Cincinnati, Ohio and I would have liked to drop in and see him and his family, but I had to continue on to New York where my wife and little daughter were waiting for me. The pull to see them was stronger than anything else. I'd waited six years. I couldn't wait another day.

Our flight time would be delayed a little as fog was pretty thick around Columbus and Washington D.C. Waiting a few hours to let the fog lift a little, our pilot took off from the Columbus, Ohio field for Washington D.C. Of course, all the ex-POWs aboard the DC 47 were getting used to air travel although most of the men were getting a little worn out. The constant movement, the noise of the engines, the stops and starts...it was exhausting in a different way than the prison camp had been.

Food was served by a N.A.T.S. female attendant, who made everybody feel at home and was a credit to the N.A.T.S. organization. She was kind and patient with us, never showing any sign of disgust at how we ate, how we hoarded food in our pockets, how we flinched at sudden movements. She had a lot of paper bills, which everybody autographed, and the finished article was called a "short snorter bill." I signed mine carefully, my hand still shaky from malnutrition.

Some very interesting sights would be observed as soon as our DC 47 approached the District of Columbia. The first object that came into view was the Potomac River and it looked very beautiful from the air. I pressed my face to the window like a child. Everything looked so clean, so undamaged. No bomb craters. No burned-out buildings. No twisted steel girders reaching toward the sky like skeletal fingers.

Subdivisions of new apartment houses were seen very near the Capitol buildings and we flew comparatively low over them. The White House could be plainly seen and it was an interesting sight. I thought about President Roosevelt, who the Japanese had called the "World's Greatest Liar." He was dead now, had died in April while we were still prisoners. We'd heard about it through the grapevine, and some of the men had wept. Now Truman was president, and the war was over, and I was going home.

Our radio operator had the news for all the passengers that two B-29s were attempting to set a new long distance record from some place in Northern Japan to Washington D.C. Not very long after landing, the two B-29s were observed near one of the hangers and apparently their flight was a success. Those magnificent planes. I thought about the raids on Osaka, the terror they'd brought to the Japanese, the hope they'd brought to us. We'd cheered silently in our bunks every time we heard the air raid sirens.

Quite a few passengers would leave the DC 47, as their destination had been reached. I watched them go, saw them embraced by waiting families. Some men broke down completely, sobbing in their wives' arms. Others stood stiff and awkward, as if they'd forgotten how to be touched with kindness.

About one hour more would elapse before another plane would be ready to take any ex-POW on to New York. Climbing aboard another DC 47, the last leg of all the ex-POWs' flight from Tokyo to New York would be ended in a matter of hours. My orders had read to report to Sampson Naval Hospital, New York for indisposition. But first, I would see my family.

Landing at Floyd Bennett field in New York, I was able to secure a room by the courtesy of the Medical officer Naval Air Station, Floyd Bennett Field, New York. I barely slept that night. I kept thinking about Jeanette, about Valerie, about what I would say, how I would act. Would they recognize me? I'd lost so much weight. My face was gaunt, my eyes sunken. I looked like a skeleton with skin stretched over it.

Next morning after breakfast a station wagon transported me to the New York, New Haven, and Hartford R.R. and at 12:00, I would be able to catch a train. I was very close to returning to the arms of my dear wife and daughter of whom I had not seen for six years. My hands were shaking as I boarded the train. I found a seat by the window and watched the countryside roll past.

Many thoughts were running through my head of how my wife would look and how she would recognize me after so long an absence. Would she be disappointed? Would she be frightened by what the war had done to me? As to my little daughter, what a sight it was going to be. She was six years old and I had never seen her, except for pictures.

How do you explain to a six-year-old where you've been, what you've seen, why you couldn't come home?

I was very tired from the long trip from Tokyo to New York and was also keyed up and under a strain. Every mile brought me closer, but it also brought more anxiety. I'd survived the war, survived the prison camp, survived the beatings and the starvation and the humiliation. But could I survive being a husband again? A father?

I was continually asking the conductors in the coach, "How much further?" and he kept saying, "Only a little way to go." The conductor was patient with me, probably used to dealing with returning servicemen. He'd seen plenty of us by now, all asking the same question, all desperate to get home.

I would also have to change at Syracuse, New York and take a bus to reach Auburn, New York, where my wife and daughter were residing. Leaving the train at Syracuse, I put in a telephone call informing my wife I would arrive in Auburn, New York at 8:55 p.m.

"I'll be there," she said. "We'll both be there."

"Jeannie," I said, and then couldn't say anything else.

"I know," she said softly. "I know, Frank. Just come home."

The bus ride seemed to take forever. I watched the sun set through the window, painting the sky in shades of orange and pink. It reminded me of the sunsets over Manila Bay, before the war, when everything was still normal. When I was still just a ship's cook on the Yangtze River Patrol, worried about nothing more than getting the crew's supper out on time.

They were there. Jeanette in a blue dress, her hair the way I remembered. A small girl beside her with dark hair who didn't know me.

The bus door opened and I stepped down. Jeanette walked toward me fast and then we were holding each other and I couldn't say anything. I just held on. She smelled like home. I didn't know what home smelled like until right then.

When I finally looked down, Valerie had stepped back behind her mother's leg and was watching me with serious eyes.

I crouched down. "Hello, Valerie."

She looked at me for a long time. Six years old. She'd never seen me except in photographs and I didn't look much like those photographs anymore.

"Are you my daddy?"

"Yes."

She thought about it. Then she put her hand in mine. Small fingers. I held them carefully, the way you hold something you're not sure you have the right to touch.

We stood there in the bus station in Auburn, New York. The three of us. After six years I didn't have words for it and I didn't try to find any.

I was home.

| 21 |

After the Kitchen Fell Silent

The last time I saw my grandfather truly himself was Christmas 1979. He stood in Grandmother's kitchen, the same kitchen where I'd first listened to his stories ten years earlier, but something had shifted. The knives weren't quite as sharp. His movements weren't quite as precise. He stood at the counter, dicing onions. His hands hesitated mid-cut, as if searching for muscle memory that had begun to fade. Alzheimer's had already started.

He still insisted on cooking. That never left him, not at first. The need to feed people, to make sure no one left his table hungry, never left him. But the precision slipped. The timing went off. He checked the same pot three times in five minutes. He reached for the salt and his hand hovered, as if he couldn't quite remember what he had reached for.

I didn't help him that Christmas. I kept to the edges of the room while the family argued. I watched and stayed quiet, an introverted teenager withdrawing into the only safe place I knew: withdrawal and silence. He cooked while the noise rose and fell around him. I kept my distance.

He didn't talk much anymore. The stories thinned out, details dropping away. Shanghai blurred. The names of shipmates drifted loose and scattered. Even Manila, the city of capture and fire, slipped into fog. But the hunger stayed.

"Make sure there's enough," he said, repeatedly, urgency in his voice. "Make sure everyone gets enough. Can't let them go hungry."

"There's plenty, Grandpa," someone said from the table. "Three turkeys, two hams, enough sides to feed an army."

"Not enough," he said, hands shaking as he reached for another pan. "Never enough. I have to make more."

Only then did I understand what I had missed in earlier years, when his mind still held together. The abundance wasn't just generosity. It was defense. Every overloaded plate, every second helping he pressed on you, every extra dish he kept in reserve was a way of fighting back against something he couldn't name.

The disease took him slowly. First it took the recent things...breakfast, yesterday's visit, the turn of the calendar. Then it took the middle years...postwar jobs, his children's names, the street where he lived. Then it took the war years...the camps, the guards, the beatings, the slow starvation that almost killed him. The kitchen outlasted them all.

I didn't see him again after that Christmas. Life pulled me in other directions, and the disease pulled him away from himself. He stayed at home, surrounded by the rooms where he had worked and rested and fed us all. The family locked the doors at night for safety, but during the day he hovered in the doorway, checking, arranging, making sure. He kept moving through the motions even when the reasons were gone.

He died January 18, 1985. The disease had taken the man long before it took his body.

I didn't go to his funeral. The family gathered and said all the right things. They talked about his Navy years, the Yangtze Patrol, his time as a POW. They talked about duty, discipline, and perseverance. All true. But none of it reached the core of who he was. Nobody mentioned the kitchen.

They didn't say how he watched plates like a sentry, how he filled them past sense, how feeding people let him fight back against guards who once rationed hunger. They didn't say that abundance was defiance. They didn't say that kindness, for him, was a weapon he never surrendered.

I never stood at his grave. I've only seen the photograph—the stone cut neat and clean, the grass around it kept short. It bears the line:

Franklin M. Hoeffer, US Navy, 1914–1985. Husband. Father. Grandfather.

True, but incomplete. It doesn't tell you about Shanghai nights or the storm through the Formosan Straits. It doesn't tell you about Manila burning, Bataan falling, or the hell ships to Japan. It doesn't tell you about Osaka or the Boy Corporal or the air raids that should have killed them. It doesn't tell you about the hunger that shaped the decades after. It doesn't tell you about the kitchen.

I thought about the leather chair and the folding chair. About a seventeen-year-old who asked questions no one else asked and received answers no one else carried. About the trust he placed in me when he told me things he told no one else.

He gave me all of it...the horror, the stubborn refusal to die, the small mercies, the quiet oaths. Alzheimer's took the man piece by piece, but not before he handed the stories to someone who would hold them.

No one leaves this table hungry.

| 22 |

Appendix: Vessels and Stations

This record outlines Franklin M. Hoeffer's U.S. Navy service from 1931 to 1952, including active duty, assignment, and captivity.

April 1, 1931 – August 16, 1931 –
U.S. Naval Training Station, Great Lakes, Illinois

August 17, 1931 – February 1, 1933 –
USS Tennessee (BB-43) – Battleship

February 2, 1933 – March 15, 1935 –
U.S. Naval Air Station Moffett Field, Sunnyvale, California

March 15, 1935 – April 10, 1935 – USS Texas (BB-35) –
Battleship

May 3, 1935 – June 12, 1935 –
U.S. Submarine Base, New London, Connecticut

June 14, 1935 – June 30, 1935 – USS Bushnell (AS-2) –
Submarine Tender

July 3, 1935 – July 2, 1936 – USS Narwhal (SS-167) –
Submarine

July 5, 1936 – July 7, 1937 – USS Holland (AS-3) –
Submarine Tender

July 3, 1937 – August 8, 1939 –
U.S. Submarine Base, New London, Connecticut

August 9, 1939 – September 10, 1939 –
USS Chaumont (AP-5) – Transport Ship
September 11, 1939 – December 4, 1939 –
USS Destroyer Base, San Diego, California
December 5, 1939 – January 5, 1940 –
USS Henderson (AP-1) – Transport Ship
January 7, 1940 – February 3, 1942 – USS *Oahu* (PR-6) –
River Gunboat *(Captured February 1942)*
May 1942 – September 1942 –
Cabanatuan Prison Camp, Philippines (Prisoner of War)
November 1942 – September 8, 1945 –
Osaka Japan Prison Camp (Prisoner of War, liberated
September 1945)
September 9, 1945 – December 10, 1945 –
U.S. Naval Hospital, Oakland, California
December 19, 1945 – March 29, 1946 –
U.S. Naval Hospital, Sampson, New York
April 4, 1946 – December 8, 1946 –
U.S. Navy Commissary Store, San Diego, California
December 19, 1946 – January 15, 1949 –
U.S. Naval Air Missile Test Center, Point Mugu, California
June 19, 1949 – June 29, 1950 – USS Nereus (AS-17) –
Submarine Tender
July 1, 1950 – August 3, 1950 –
USS LST-1084 (Landing Ship, Tank)
August 10, 1950 – September 15, 1950 –
U.S. Naval Receiving Station, San Francisco, California
September 25, 1950 – January 3, 1951 –
U.S. Naval Station, San Diego, California
November 30, 1951 – April 10, 1952 –
USS Weeden (DE-797) – Destroyer Escort

| 23 |

About the Author

Richard Lowe is a professional ghostwriter who has helped Fortune 50 executives and thought leaders tell their stories. His clients have secured over $30 million in venture capital using books he helped create.

Before his writing career, Richard spent twenty years managing technology at Trader Joe's, where he learned that feeding people well is its own form of respect.

Behind the Wire is personal. Frank Hoeffer II was his grandfather. The stories in this book came from conversations during Christmas visits in the late 1970s — captured just before Alzheimer's erased the man who lived them. Richard was the only family member who asked to hear them.

He lives in Florida.

BOOKS BY RICHARD LOWE

See books by Richard Lowe at
https://masterofworlds.com

Get free publishing insights and industry updates at
https://thewritingking.substack.com

For ghostwriting and book coaching services see
https://thewritingking.com